TV
Towns

Stephen Tropiano

 Books

New York

Library of Congress Cataloging-in-Publication Data available upon request from publisher.

All photos courtesy of Photofest.

The publisher has made every effort to secure permission to reproduce copyrighted material and would like to apologize should there have been any errors or omissions.

TV Books, L.L.C.
1619 Broadway, Ninth Floor
New York, NY 10019
www.tvbooks.com

Interior design by Deborah Daly
Manufactured in the United States of America

Contents

Introduction	7
Bedrock *(The Flintstones)*	8
Cabot Cove, Maine *(Murder, She Wrote)*	16
Capeside, Massachusetts *(Dawson's Creek)*	24
Central City *(The Many Loves of Dobie Gillis)*	30
Cicely, Alaska *(Northern Exposure)*	36
Collinsport, Maine *(Dark Shadows)*	44
Fernwood, Ohio *(Mary Hartman, Mary Hartman;*	
Forever Fernwood; Fernwood 2night)	52
Gilligan's Island *(Gilligan's Island)*	58
Gotham City *(Batman)*	66
Hazzard, Georgia *(The Dukes of Hazzard)*	74
Hooterville *(Petticoat Junction; Green Acres)*	80
A little town in Vermont *(Newhart)*	88
Llanview, Pennsylvania *(One Life to Live)*	94
Mayberry, North Carolina *(The Andy Griffith Show; Mayberry, R.F.D.)*	100
Mayfield *(Leave It to Beaver; Still the Beaver; The New Leave It to Beaver)*	108
Orbit City *(The Jetsons)*	116
Peyton Place *(Peyton Place; Return to Peyton Place)*	122
Port Charles, New York *(General Hospital; Port Charles)*	128
Salem *(Days of Our Lives)*	136
Springfield *(The Simpsons)*	144
Twin Peaks, Washington *(Twin Peaks)*	152
Sources	159
Websites	160

Introduction

I grew up in Verplanck, New York, a small suburban town on the Hudson River in Westchester County. Both Verplanck and the neighboring village of Buchanan, where my family moved when I was eight, were terrific places to live. The people were friendly, the streets were safe, and, on the whole, life was simple, peaceful, and at times, a little bit dull.

Television provided me with an escape from the boredom of suburbia. I became an avid TV watcher at a very young age (just ask anyone in my family!). Like most people, my first exposure to the outside world was through my favorite television programs. I had no reason to believe that Mayberry, Hooterville, and Collinsport were not real places and that Opie Taylor, Lisa Douglas, and Barnabas Collins were not real people. I was envious because unlike Verplanck, there was always something happening in the towns on television. And I felt I was missing out.

Now I am older, a little wiser, and can distinguish (well, at least most of the time) between what's real and what's not. I am still an avid TV watcher. Although I have less time to devote to television, I will stop what I am doing to tune into my favorite episodes of some of the programs I watched religiously when I was younger. They never fail to take me back to the TV towns where I lived as a kid. I wrote this book to preserve that feeling and to share with other TV fans that which we love to remember—and maybe even have forgotten—about our favorite television towns, both past and present.

For their assistance and support with this book, thanks to Grant Rickard, Rob Meunier, Ilka Rivard, Christine Tucci and Vincent Angell, Faith Ginsberg, Linda Bobel, Jeff and Shelly Bergen, Arnold Stiefel, Craig Ferguson, Robert Parrish, Claudia Lamb, Patty Zimmermann, Robin Jones, Matthew Beck, Albert DePetrillo at TV Books, my friends at SEFAL, Tom Bohn, and my current TV-watching partner, Steven Ginsberg. A special thanks to all my friends in cyberspace who provide me with information and the folks at the best video store in the world, Eddie Brandt's Saturday Matinee in North Hollywood, California.

The process of researching and writing this book took me back to a time in my life when watching television was more than a pasttime—it was a passion. Some of my earliest and best childhood memories involve watching some of my favorite television shows, like *Batman* and *Dark Shadows*, with my older brothers, Michael and Joe. This book is dedicated to them, to my parents for letting us watch, and in loving memory of Marion Skolnick.

Stephen Tropiano
stevetrop@aol.com
Los Angeles, California

7

Bedrock

The Flintstones (1960–66)

Created by William Hanna and Joseph Barbera

The first animated situation comedy, *The Flintstones,* has been an important part of American television culture since it debuted in September 1960. In the vision of the series' creators, William Hanna and Joseph Barbera, life during the Stone Age was far from primitive, at least in Bedrock, the hometown of Fred, Wilma, and Pebbles Flintstone, the modern Stone Age family that resides at 201 Cobblestone Lane. Although the Flintstones and their next door neighbors, the Rubbles—Barney, his wife Betty, and their son Bamm-Bamm—wear animal furs and live in stone houses, they may as well be living in early 1960s suburban America. *The Flintstones* celebrates the Stone Age as a civilized period in our prehistory in which people enjoyed luxuries of the twentieth century such as the automobile, the telephone, the phonograph, the refrigerator, and the motion-picture camera.

Based on Jackie Gleason's *The Honeymooners* (closely enough that Gleason considered suing), *The Flintstones* follows the antics of a working-class guy named Fred

Fred, Wilma, Pebbles, and Dino Flintstone reside at 201 Cobblestone Lane.

"Yabba-dabba-do!" It's quitting time at the Rock Head and Quarry Construction Company.

ney entertained. The boys enjoy bowling at the Bedrock Bowl (where they are members of a bowling league), shooting pool at Dan Boulder's Billiard Parlor, and playing poker. They are also members of the Royal Order of the Water Buffalo Lodge, which sponsors an annual convention as well as other events like picnics, costume parties, golf tournaments, fishing trips, and beauty contests.

In order to go bowling, watch the fights, or play poker, Fred sometimes tells Wilma a little white lie or two, which usually comes back to haunt him. When they were first married, Fred had a gambling problem, but he was cured by a psychiatrist (obviously the treatment worked because Fred still enjoys a game of cards and an occasional trip to the racetrack). He is constantly trying (and failing) to get rich quick by devising some scheme with Barney, like writing a hit song or inventing a new soft drink or buying a drive-in restaurant. Fred even had a brief acting career when movie companies from Hollyrock came to Bedrock to shoot *The Monster from the Tarpits* and *Hercurock and the Maidens*. In spite of all his faults, Fred really does love Wilma and wants to give her a better life. He occasionally goes out of his way for her, taking dance lessons (at the Arthur Quarry Dance School) or buying her a piano for their anniversary. Both the Flintstones and the Rubbles frequent Bedrock's many nightclubs, such as the Rockadero and the Copa Cave, and the city's more expensive restaurants, like the Piltdown Hotel Supper Club and the Chateau Rockinbleu.

who operates a dinosaur crane in a gravel pit for the Rock Head and Quarry Construction Company. Like Ralph Kramden, Fred is loud, overweight, and has a short temper. He is always unsuccessful when he tries to impress his boss, Mr. Slate, or hatches one of his get-rich-quick schemes. Beneath his gruff exterior, Fred actually has a big heart. He is a devoted husband and father and a loyal friend to his neighbor, Barney, who bears a close resemblance to Kramden's best friend and neighbor, Ed Norton.

Bedrock (population 2,500) is a relatively small suburban community located 250 feet below sea level in Cobblestone County. There is plenty in town to keep Fred and Bar-

Did You Know?

The Flintstones often appeared in animated commercials for their sponsors, which included Miles Laboratories (makers of Alka Seltzer and One-A-Day vitamins) and Winston cigarettes.

- In an ad for Winston cigarettes, Wilma is mowing the lawn and Betty is beating a rug, while Fred and Barney sit on the side of the house enjoying a Winston cigarette break.

- The characters appeared in a twenty-five minute animated short produced by Hanna-Barbera and the Gardner Advertising Company for the Anheuser-Busch Company to introduce distributors to their 1967 "target" media advertising campaign (along with the new ad line, "When you're due for a beer, Busch does it!"). Fred and Barney are shown relaxing at their favorite watering hole, The Grove, and watching an industry film on television outlining Busch's upcoming ad campaign.

There are many inconsistencies in the series regarding the names of people and places:

- Fred works at the Rockhead and Quarry Cave Construction Company, also known as the Bedrock Slate and Gravel Company.

- His boss is Mr. Slate, though sometimes it's Mr. Granite or Mr. Rockhead.

- The Flintstones live at 201 Cobblestone Lane, but several other addresses are given: 323 Cobblestone Lane, 342 Greasepit Terrace, 342 Gravel Pit Terrace, 55 Cobblestone Road, 34 Cobblestone Road, and 201 Cobblestone Way.

Wilma Slaghoople Flintstone is a modern housewife who is very practical and extremely patient, particularly when dealing with her husband. She loves to shop and can often be heard yelling "Charge it!" when she and best friend Betty are heading toward Macyrock Department Store. Wilma is also starstruck and falls apart in the presence of movie stars like Rock Quarry and Stony Curtis. Like Fred, she came close to becoming a celebrity herself when she was chosen by TV producer Norman Rockbind to star in a commercial for Softly Skin Lotion (Betty actually ended up starring in the commercial). When Wilma worked at the Bedrock Radio and Television Corporation she became the host of a homemaker show, *The Happy Housewife Show* (sponsored by Rockenschpeel Fine Foods), which left husband Fred feeling very neglected (and hungry at dinner time).

Wilma and Fred's life would change forever on February 22, 10,000 B.C., when daughter Pebbles was born at the Bedrock Rockapedic Hospital. Shortly after, the Rubbles decided to adopt Bamm-Bamm, who was left on their doorstep. Fred and Barney are both attentive fathers who participate in PTA activities, such as playing the title roles in the PTA's production of *Romeorock and Julietstone*. They also take their families to see the performing sealosauraus at Oceanrock Aquarium, enjoy the afternoon at Bedrock's amusement park, Bedrock-land, and whoop it up at the Bedrock Rodeo (where Fred did a brief stint as a rodeo clown). Becoming fathers didn't limit Fred and Barney's freedom to go out and spend time with the boys. They joined the Daddies Anonymous Club, where they could enjoy a game of cards with other Bedrock fathers as they babysat for their kids.

The Flintstones and the Rubbles are constantly struggling to move up the eco-nomic ladder, yet when they get the chance to rub elbows with Bedrock's elite, they always learn the same simple lesson—be yourself. Once Fred moved his family into a mansion in an upscale neighborhood, but they returned to Cobblestone Lane when he and Wilma discovered that their neighbors were freeloading snobs. Another time Fred took a custodial job so his family could live in a ritzy apartment building, the Bedrock Towers. The Flintstones soon learned that there is nothing glamorous about living in the basement of a building and being hounded all day long by disgruntled tenants. When the two couples attended a white-tie ambassador's reception instead of the annual fire-

Once again in search for stardom, Fred Flintstone poses outside of the Cinerock Dome.

man's ball, they felt uncomfortable mingling with the social climbers of Bedrock until Fred won them over by capturing a jewel thief.

Bedrock has played host to several famous visitors. Ann-Margrock (guest voice Ann-Margret) came to town to appear in the Bedrock Bowl Amphitheater. Unaware of her identity, the Flintstones hired her to baby-sit Pebbles. Stoney Curtis (guest voice Tony Curtis) arrived to make his new film, *Slave Boy*, and gave a job to Fred, who discovered that being a stand-in is a less than glamorous job. Bedrock has also been invaded by aliens, including ten robots resembling Fred and a little green man named Gazoo (guest voice Harvey Korman) from the Planet Zetox. Gazoo befriended Barney and Fred (who he referred to as "dumb-dumbs") and in several episodes offered them advice and some magical assistance.

The Flintstones and Rubbles frequently venture out of Bedrock for vacation. They first visited their favorite spot, Hollyrock, when Wilma and Betty won a TV slogan contest. Wilma got a part on a television show, *The Frogmouth*, playing the wife of an overbearing husband who is played by none other than Fred. The women won another contest and headed to Rockiki beach to meet their TV idol, Larry Lava, star of *Hawaiian Eye*. Once again, Fred got a job on the show, this time as a stuntman. The couple also visited Fred's rich Uncle Tex in Texarock, fell victim to two con artists in Rock Vegas, got involved with diamond thieves in Rockapulco, and attended the Water Buffalo convention in Frantic City.

After *The Flintstones* left prime time in 1966, reruns appeared on Saturday mornings on all three networks. Hanna-Barbera eventually produced new cartoons, including *The Pebbles and Bamm-Bamm Show*, in which the offspring of the Flintstones and the Rubbles were teenagers attending Bedrock High School and playing in a (what else?) rock band. Another incarnation, *The Flintstones Kids*, depicted Fred, Barney, Wilma, and Betty as adolescents.

The Flintstones also made it to the big screen, first in an animated feature, *The Man Called Flintstone* (1966), and more recently, in two live-action films, *The Flintstones* (1994) and a prequel, *The Flintstones in Viva Rock Vegas* (2000), which focuses on how Fred and Barney met Wilma and Betty. Both films have turned a whole new generation onto television's favorite modern Stone Age family.

RECOMMENDED VIEWING

To get a feel for life in Bedrock, the following episodes are recommended viewing:

"The Drive-In"
Writer: Warren Foster
Tired of their routine jobs, Fred and Barney buy a drive-in restaurant without telling their wives. When two cute carhops call Fred's house to ask for jobs, Wilma and Betty become suspicious. Original airdate: 12/23/60

"Arthur Quarry's Dance Class"
Writer: Warren Foster
Wilma and Betty get free tickets to a charity dance, but Fred and Barney don't know how to dance. The husbands join Joe Rockhead's Volunteer Fire Department, which gives them an excuse to go out every night and take dance lessons at Arthur Quarry's Dance School. Original airdate: 1/13/61

"Tycoon"
Writer: Warren Foster
Fred assumes the identity of his double, tycoon J.L. Gutrocks, who goes off to find out what it's like to live an ordinary life. Wilma and the Rubbles mistake Gutrocks for Fred, while the real Fred discovers it's no picnic being the head of a financial empire. *Note: the episode begins with a panoramic view of the city of Bedrock.* Original airdate: 2/24/61

The Flintstones

Premiere Airdate: September 30, 1960
ABC   166 Episodes

The Original Voices

Fred Flintstone	. . . . Alan Reed	Betty Rubble	. . . . Bea Benaderet (1960–64)
Wilma Flintstone	. . . . Jean Vander Pyl		. . . . Gerry Johnson (1964–65)
Barney Rubble	. . . . Mel Blanc		

Jessica (Angela Lansbury) takes time out on her visit into town to chat with Dr. Seth Hazlitt (William Windom).

Cabot Cove, Maine

Murder, She Wrote (1984–96)

Created by Peter Fischer and Richard Levinson and William Link

---

Cabot Cove at a Glance

Where to Stay:
- The Hill House Inn $$$
- The Lighthouse Motel $$
- The Starlite Motel $
- The Paradise Motel $

Where to Dine:
- The Joshua Peabody Inn $$$
- The Cabot Cove Diner $$
- The Cabot Cove Coffee Shop $

Where to Shop:
- Castle Cove Bookstore
- The antique stores on Main Street

Local Newspaper:
- *The Cabot Cove Gazette*

Local Holiday:
- Founder's Day (in November)

Historical Attraction:
- Joshua Peabody Homestead and Museum

The idyllic New England town of Cabot Cove, Maine, is the setting for this long-running "whodunit" series. Angela Lansbury stars as Jessica Fletcher, a substitute English teacher at Cabot Cove High School who loves reading murder mysteries. In the series pilot, Jessica writes a mystery for fun and, thanks to her nephew Grady, the manuscript lands on the desk of a New York publisher. *The Corpse Danced at Midnight* is an overnight success and Jessica, writing under the pen name J.B. Fletcher, becomes one of the country's most popular and highly-respected mystery writers.

Curious and observant, Jessica has a nose for trouble. Whether she is home in Cabot Cove or traveling around the world, she is always ready and willing to assist the authorities with solving a murder and apprehending the killer. Jessica is usually one step ahead of the police, who have no choice to but to take a back seat to the master sleuth. During the series' twelve-year run, Mrs. Fletcher solved over 261 cases and still managed to find the time to write twenty-eight mysteries!

Jessica's hometown, Cabot Cove, is a

small fishing village located on Route 1, which runs along the Atlantic coast up to the Maine-New Brunswick border. The center of this quaint, picturesque town is Main Street, which rests along the waterfront. The street is lined with local businesses and shops, including a motel, an outdoor café, a bookshop, and several antique stores. Every morning you can see the town's local celebrity, who refuses to learn how to drive a car, riding her bicycle from her home at 698 Candlewood Lane into the center of town.

Cabot Cove's founder, Joshua Peabody, was a clockmaker and Revolutionary War hero who led the Battle of Cabot Cove in 1780. For many years, a reenactment of the battle was part of the annual Founder's Day Celebration, which is held in November. Peabody's loyalty to the American side was called into question when a letter from George Washington accusing him of being a traitor was found in an antique music box. Jessica proved the letter was a fake, which pleased both the Peabody family, who operate the Joshua Peabody Homestead and Museum, and Cabot Cove shop owners, who depend on the town's history to attract tourists. The remains of Joshua Peabody were believed to have been found during the digging for a high-rise building, but it was never proven they belonged to him. In fact, some folks even question whether Peabody really existed at all.

Another Founder's Day celebration was disrupted when the townspeople learned that Cabot Cove was built on land still legally owned by the Algonquin Indians. A man claiming to be the descendant of a chieftain named Manitoka arrived in town to prove that the land was given to his ancestor by the British for helping them win a major battle against the French. The document was authentic, but before he could begin collecting rent on every home and business in the town, Jessica proved that the visitor's claim to be the eleventh descendant of the chieftain was inconclusive.

Did You Know?

Jean Stapleton, *All in the Family's* Edith Bunker, was originally slated to play the role of Jessica Fletcher. After reading the script of the two-hour pilot, she felt it wasn't for her and turned it down. The part was then offered to Angela Lansbury.

Murder, She Wrote was not the first time Angela Lansbury portrayed a detective. She starred as Miss Jane Marple in the 1980 film version of Agatha Christie's *The Mirror Crack'd.*

A former MGM contract player, Lansbury created an opportunity to work with other actors from the Hollywood studio era. The roster of stars who appeared in the series included Mickey Rooney, Cesar Romero, June Allyson, Van Johnson, Cyd Charisse, Mel Ferrer, Ruth Roman, Gloria DeHaven, Kathryn Grayson, Roddy McDowall, and Carroll Baker.

Sheriff Tupper (Tom Bosley), Jessica Fletcher (Angela Lansbury), and Dr. Hazlitt (William Windom) on their way to the scene of yet another Cabot Cove murder.

Cabot Cove, Maine, in Mendocino, California

Hill House Inn
10701 Palette Drive

Visitors to Cabot Cove choose to stay at the Hill House Inn, which is a real inn located near downtown Mendocino. The Hill House Inn was used for both exterior and interior shots and provided lodging for the cast and crew when they were shooting on location.

Blair House
45110 Little Lake Street

The exterior of this Victorian bed and breakfast, built in 1888, was used for the exterior shots of Mrs. Fletcher's Cabot Cove home.

The tranquillity of Cabot Cove was also constantly being threatened by land developers. In several episodes, an outsider arrives in town to oversee the construction of a new building, but the real estate deal is always shady, which means someone eventually ends up with a bullet hole through his or her head. Over the years, the town was in danger of becoming the home of a cannery, a high-rise hotel project (right on Main Street), condos, a resort, and a combination residential-business complex. In the end, Cabot Cove is saved from corporate invaders by Mrs. Fletcher and the town's environ-

mentally-conscious citizens. Ironically, one of the local industries in the area (besides fishing) is a plant owned by Pantechnics—a manufacturer of guided missiles!

Jessica's best friends in Cabot Cove are the crotchety town doctor, Seth Hazlitt, and the amiable Sheriff Amos Tupper, who retired in 1988 and was replaced by Sheriff Mort Metzger. The locals are a colorful bunch. Among them are the town's long-winded mayor, Sam Booth, and two real estate agents, the greedy Harry Pierce (who did a short stint as sheriff) and man-hungry Eve Simpson. Eve is a patron of Loretta's Beauty Shop, the gathering place for the town gossips of Cabot Cove. There you will find Ideal Molloy, Phyllis Grant, and the shop's owner, Loretta Spiegel, exchanging juicy tidbits. When one of Jessica's former students penned an unflattering exposé of the town titled *The Sins of Cabot Cove*, she got the local dirt first hand from Corinne, Loretta's helper in the shop.

Although Cabot Cove appears to be a nice place to vacation or even live, one reason to keep your distance from this ocean-front hamlet is the murder rate, which is unusually high for a town with a population of 3,560. Over the course of twelve years, more than thirty Cabot Cove citizens and twenty outsiders or former town residents were murdered. Thanks to Mrs. Fletcher, all of the murders were solved (Jessica's husband, Frank, a real estate broker who died in the 1980s, seems to have been the only resident of Cabot Cove who died of nat-

Did You Know?

A Boston detective named Harry McGraw, whom Mrs. Fletcher often assisted when she traveled to the big city, was given his own series in 1987, the short-lived *The Law and Harry McGraw*. Jerry Orbach played the disorganized and grouchy private detective whose office was across the hall from his friend, a respectable lawyer named Ellie Maginnis (Barbara Babcock). The spinoff was canceled in February 1988, but Jerry Orbach would return to sleuthing four years later as New York City Detective Lennie Briscoe on *Law & Order*.

During the sixth (1989–90) and seventh (1990–91) seasons, Angela Lansbury decided to take a break from the daily grind of a weekly series. For several episodes, Jessica Fletcher only appeared in the opening and closing of the show. She would introduce the "guest detective" and set up the story. The ratings started to decline, so Jessica resumed her crime-solving duties full-time in the eight season. By the ninth season, *Murder, She Wrote* was back in the top five series.

Angela Lansbury, a three-time Tony Award winner, is the Susan Lucci of prime-time television. She has been nominated for sixteen Emmy Awards (twelve for *Murder, She Wrote*), but has never won. Hopefully, like Lucci, she will end her losing streak soon and win a much-deserved Emmy.

ural causes). One has to wonder why wherever Mrs. Fletcher is, whether it be Cabot Cove or some exotic location like Paris or the Mediterranean, a murder is committed (which makes you think Jessica would not be anyone's top choice for a houseguest).

Perhaps bored of small town life, Mrs. Fletcher made a big move at the start of the eighth season (1991–92) to New York City. She moved into an apartment on Manhattan's Upper West Side (941 West 61st Street). The former substitute teacher graduated to teaching criminology at Manhattan University. Jessica also volunteered at St. Julian's, an inner city school, where she taught a mystery-writing class. She did not abandon Cabot Cove entirely, but would travel back on weekends for some relaxation—and to solve murders.

Fortunately for the Cabot Cove Sheriff's Department, a murder would only occur when Jessica was back in town.

Murder, She Wrote was filmed on the backlot of Universal Studios in Los Angeles. If you take the backlot tram tour, you will see many of the exterior sets which were used for the series. The small wharf and the shops on Main Street are in the same area where tourgoers encounter Bruce the Shark from *Jaws*. For other exterior scenes of the New England town, the cast and crew traveled to Mendocino, a small coastal town in Northern California.

RECOMMENDED VIEWING

To get a feel for life in Cabot Cove and its quirky townspeople, the following episodes are recommended:

"Keep the Home Fries Burning"
Writer: Phillip Gerson
Director: Peter Crane

Floyd Nelson, the owner of the Joshua Peabody Inn, is stealing customers from the local diner. When patrons at the Inn suffer from food poisoning which results in one fatality, the diner's owner, Bo Dixon, is suspected of murder. Original airdate: 1/19/86

"If It's Thursday, It Must Be Beverly Hills"
Writers: Wendy Graf, Lisa Stotsky
Director: Peter Crane

When investigating one of Sheriff's Tupper's deputies, who is accused of murdering his wife, Jessica discovers the deputy has been bedding several women in Cabot Cove. This episode introduced viewers to the gossip center of Cabot Cove—Loretta Spiegel's beauty shop. Original airdate: 11/8/87

"The Sins of Cabot Cove"
Writer: Robert Van Scoyk
Director: John Llewellyn Moxey

One of Jessica's former students pens a novel entitled *The Sins of Cabot Cove*, which contains more truth than fiction about the townspeople. The book sparks a series of events, including the torching of the local bookstore and the murder of the town butcher, who was having an affair with a married woman. Original airdate: 4/9/89

"To Kill A Legend"
Writers: David Bennett Carren,
**   J. Larry Carroll**
Director: Anthony Shaw

The townspeople are reenacting the Battle of Cabot Cove for a documentary. When a letter suggesting Revolutionary War hero Joshua Peabody may have been a traitor to the British, everyone panics. By solving the murder of the film's cinematographer, Jessica manages to set history straight. Original airdate: 10/9/94

Murder, She Wrote

Premiere Airdate: September 30, 1984
CBS   261 Episodes

Cast

Jessica Beatrice Fletcher. . . . Angela Lansbury

Recurring Characters:

Sheriff Amos Tupper . . . . Tom Bosley (1984–88)
Dr. Seth Hazlitt . . . . . William Windom (1985–96)
Sheriff Mort Metzger . . . . Ron Masak (1989–96)
Mayor Sam Booth . . . . . Richard Paul (1986–91)

Grady Fletcher. . . . . . Michael Horton (1984–95)
Eve Simpson . . . . Julie Adams (1987–93)
Deputy Andy Broom   . Louis Herthum (1991–96)

Capeside, Massachusetts

Dawson's Creek (1998–Present)

Created by Kevin Williamson

A New England tourist spot on Cape Cod is the setting for this drama about the growing pains of Dawson Wade Leery, an aspiring filmmaker and avid film buff. Capeside is a picturesque, colonial town that provides an almost storybook setting for all the teenage angst experienced by Dawson and his pals. The waterfront, lined with park benches and strings of lights, is the most romantic spot in town. It's where Dawson shared a slow dance with his new neighbor, Jen Lindley, the "fast" girl with a reputation who moved to Capeside from New York City to live with her Bible-thumping grandmother. At the same time, Dawson's best friend, Pacey Witter, was locking lips with his sexy English teacher, Tamara Jacobs. Keeping the streets safe for late-night lovers are Pacey's father, Police Chief Witter, and Pacey's brother, Deputy Doug, who has a soft spot for Broadway show tunes, but denies all rumors (spread by Pacey) that he is gay.

Created by Kevin Williamson, best known for penning the *Scream* film trilogy, *Dawson's Creek* is the PG-13 version of *Beverly Hills, 90210*. Some of the situations Dawson and his friends face each week are familiar (parents getting divorced, losing your virginity, love triangles), while others have been considered by critics and TV watchdog groups as "inappropriate" for prime-time television (a teacher-student sexual relationship, teen homosexuality).

Capeside at a Glance

Where to Stay:
Potter's Bed and Breakfast

Where to Rent a Video:
Screen Play Video

Local TV Station:
WKWB-TV

The teens of Capeside (clockwise from top): Pacey (Joshua Jackson), Joey (Katie Holmes), Dawson (James Van Der Beek), and Jen (Michelle Williams).

Dawson (James Van Der Beek) and on-again/off-again girlfriend Joey Potter (Katie Holmes) catch some rays.

When they are not at school or pursuing the opposite sex, Dawson and Pacey work at Screen Play Video. The store is located right in the center of town, near shops and cafés where both the townies and tourists hang out. Its owner, Mr. Olsen, is the father of the annoying Nellie Olsen (her name is no doubt an homage to Laura Ingall's rival on *Little House on the Prairie*). Dawson is a film freak who spends every night watching films in his room, which is adorned with posters for *Jaws, Hook, Close Encounters, and Jurassic Park*. Spielberg is Dawson's favorite director, though a poster for Williamson's *Scream* and

I Know What You Did Last Summer have also appeared on the walls of Capeside High School. His childhood friend, Joey Potter, usually rows her boat across the creek to Dawson's backyard and climbs up a ladder to his window to join him for a late night video-watching session and to engage in some heavy conversations about sex, love, and high school. Dawson takes his film watching very seriously, so he mourned the closing of Capeside's old Rialto Theater—his favorite place to watch a movie.

A popular hangout in Capeside is the SS *Icehouse*, where Joey Potter works with her sister Bessie. At the Icehouse, patrons can sit outside at picnic tables and enjoy burgers and seafood. Joey's drug dealing father took over the place when he was released from jail, but not for long: one of his unsatisfied "customers" set the Icehouse on fire. Until the Icehouse is rebuilt, the gang may have to hang out at one of the local clubs, which is where the underage Dawson celebrated his birthday by having one too many rum and cokes and singing the blues on stage. For something a little more upscale, there's the Capeside Yacht Club and Marina, which sponsors the annual Miss Windjammer Pageant.

Capeside is a small town, but does have a local television station, WKWB-TV, where Dawson's mother, Gail, worked as a reporter. Her job and her marriage to Dawson's father, Mitch, ended when she became romantically involved with Bob, the local anchorman. Meanwhile, Mitch became coach of the Capeside Football Team, which ended its losing streak thanks to the openly gay quarterback, Jack McPhee. Jack and his sister Andie, who suffered a nervous breakdown, moved to Capeside during the 1998–99 season.

Capeside, Massachusetts, in Wilmington, North Carolina

Dawson's Creek is filmed in Wilmington, a historic eighteenth-century town located on North Carolina's Cape Fear Coast, and Southport, a fishing village thirty miles to the south. The interiors are filmed at EUE/Screen Gems Studios (1223 N. 23rd Street), which is the largest production facility east of Hollywood. Several of the businesses in Wilmington double for locations used in *Dawson's*, including The Icehouse (115 S. Water Street) and Screen Play Video (118 Princess Street). Additional locations include Mollye's Market (118 Princess Street), where characters like to have a bite to eat, and Thalian Hall Center for the Performing Arts (310 Chestnut Street), which doubled for the interior of the Rialto Theater. Exterior sequences along the water are shot at the Cape Fear Riverwalk (on Market Street) and Riverfront Park (on Water Street). The exterior sequences of Capeside High School are shot at nearby University of North Carolina at Wilmington.

RECOMMENDED VIEWING

To get a feel for life in Capeside, the following episodes are recommended:

"Blown Away"
Writer: Jon Harmon Feldman
Director: Steve Miner

A hurricane roars into Capeside, though the real storm is inside the Leery home, where Dawson forces his mother to admit she's having an affair. Original airdate: 2/17/98

"The Breakfast Club"
Writer: Mike White
Director: Allan Arkush

In an homage to John Hughes' 1985 brat pack comedy-drama, Dawson, Pacey, Joey, Jen, and Abby find themselves in Saturday detention, under the watchful eye of Mrs. Tingle. Original airdate: 3/3/98

Did You Know?

During the first season, film titles were used as episode titles.

The list included *Dirty Dancing, Carnal Knowledge, Blown Away, Escape From New York, Modern Romance, In the Company of Men, Look Who's Talking,* and *The Breakfast Club.* Perhaps to avoid legal problems, original titles were used during the second season.

Pacey (Joshua Jackson) takes some time out to relax.

"Friday the 13th"
Writer: Mike White
Director: Rodman Flender

In an homage to Williamson's own *Scream*, it's Halloween in Capeside, where there's a serial killer on the loose, which puts Dawson and the gang on edge as they celebrate at Dawson's house. Original airdate: 5/5/98

Dawson's Creek

Premiere Airdate: January 20, 1998
WB Network

Cast

Dawson Leery . . . . James Van Der Beek	Mitch Leery . . . . John Wesley Shipp
Joey Potter . . . . Katie Holmes	Mary Beth Peil . . . . Gail Leery
Jen Lindley . . . . Michelle Williams	Bessie Potter . . . . Nina Repeta
Pacey Witter . . . . Joshua Jackson	Andie McPhee . . . . Meredith Monroe
Grams . . . . Mary Margaret Humes	Jack McPhee . . . . Kerr Smith

---

Central City

The Many Loves of Dobie Gillis (1959–63)

Created by Max Shulman

Dobie Gillis is the all-American teenager with only one thing on his mind—girls. All Dobie wants (in his words) is "one beautiful, gorgeous, soft, round, creamy girl" for his very own. Every day, Dobie sits in the park in his hometown, Central City, in front of Rodin's statue "The Thinker." He strikes a similar pose as he ponders the complexities of life, which basically boil down to how a guy with no money can get a girl who only wants a guy with money.

Based on characters created by Max Shulman, Dobie lives in Central City with his father Herbert, mother Winnie, and his rarely seen older brother Davey. The town is essentially located in Anywhere, U.S.A. (the only clue that the town is west of the Mississippi is that the call letters of the local TV station, KMST-TV, begin with a K). Unlike most television towns of the 1950s and early 1960s, which either belong to little kids (like Beaver and Dennis the Menace) or the adults (like the good folks of Mayberry), Central City was ruled by teenagers—Dobie, his beatnik pal Maynard, the money-hungry

---

Central City at a Glance

Where to Stay:
   The Palace Hotel $$$$

Where to Dine:
   Charlie Wong's Ice Cream Parlor $

Where to Shop:
   Gillis' Groceries
   Riff Ryan's Record Shop
   Ralph T. Ziegler Men's Clothing

Local Newspaper:
   The Daily Courier

Local Media:
   KMST-TV

At the beginning of each episode, Dobie Gillis (Dwayne Hickman) assumes "The Thinker" pose in Central City Park.

Thalia Menninger, snobby Milton Armitage, rich kid Chatsworth Osborne, and the brainy Zelda Gilroy.

What little viewers saw of Central City revolved around the daily life of the "average" American teenager. During the first few seasons, Dobie and his friends were students at Central City High School. After graduation, Dobie and Maynard enlisted for a brief stint in the army. When they were honorably discharged, they decided to enroll in S. Peter Pryor Junior College.

When they are not in school, Dobie and his pals hang out at Charlie Wong's Ice Cream Parlor. Wong's features 31 Celestial Flavors

Did You Know?

Dwayne Hickman's hair was lightened to make him look younger in the beginning of the series, but his natural hair color eventually grew in.

Bob Denver was drafted early in the series and was replaced for a short time by Michael J. Pollard, who played his cousin Jerome. Maynard's departure from the series was explained by Maynard's joining the army. Denver had broken his vertebra in a car accident when he was younger, so he was released from duty as 4-F and returned immediately to the series. Pollard's character was written out of the show.

Dobie loved Thalia, but there was no love lost between Dwayne Hickman and his co-star Tuesday Weld, who left the series after the first season and returned for a brief stint at the beginning of the fourth. At the time she first appeared on the show, the sexy Weld was considered an up-and-coming star and gained more attention than she could handle from the press and the media. Her stardom would later be surpassed by co-star Warren Beatty, who appeared as a regular in the 1959–60 season.

Dobie (Dwayne Hickman) and Zelda (Sheila James) hang out in Charles Wong's Ice Cream Parlor, where proprietor Charlie (John Lee) offers specials like the Strawberry Won-Ton Sundae.

and specials like the Strawberry Won-Ton Sundae. (A Chinese store owner and a Mexican milkman, Senior Carlos, with whom Mrs. Gillis converses in Spanish, suggests there is some racial diversity in Central City). The parlor has a piano, where Maynard likes to sit and bang out tunes. Another place to pass the time is the Bijou Movie Theater, which holds "Jackpot Night" every week. If the number on your ticket is called, you win one hundred dollars. Ironically, this is one of the gimmicks movie theaters used in the 1950s to get back their audiences, who were home watching television.

One place Dobie would never be found is working in his father's store, Gillis' Groceries, at 285 Norwood Street, where the Gillis family lives over the store. Dobie is always asking for money or swiping some from the store register, but he doesn't want to work for it. Herbert Gillis, who has a short temper, thinks his son is lazy ("I'm gonna kill that boy!" he repeatedly cries). Winnie Gillis defends her son, whom she thinks is bright, sensitive, and acting like every other seven-

Zelda Gilroy (Sheila James) serenades her future husband Dobie Gillis (Dwayne Hickman).

teen-year-old. On the rare occasion that Dobie is left in charge of the store, something usually goes wrong because he lets his libido get the best of him. The manipulative Thalia, who is determined to marry money, thinks Dobie has the potential to make it rich. To help him along the way, she hatches schemes—like making 400 ham and cheese sandwiches to sell at the high school picnic at

Cedar Lake, only to have the event rained out (and Dobie's father stuck with the bill).

Work was also the last thing on the mind of television's first weekly beatnik character, Maynard G. Krebs (the "G" stands for Walter). Maynard is TV's version of a nonconformist. He sports a goatee, wears the same two ripped sweatshirts, and uses expressions like "cool," "cat," and "dig." Maynard loves jazz and plays the trumpet in the Central High School band, though he has a tendency to improvise. He also has a keen sense of hearing and is a bit accident-prone (the Red Cross considered declaring him a disaster area). Maynard knows the other beats in town, including Riff Ryan, owner of Riff Ryan's Record Shop, where he meets a female beat, known only as "Far-Out Girl."

The one woman in Dobie's life who truly believes in him is a tomboy named Zelda. She signals her love to Dobie by calling him "Poopsie" and wrinkling her nose at him, causing him to involuntarily wrinkle his nose back. Zelda is confident that she and Dobie will one day be married, so she takes an interest in his future (so they won't starve to death, she makes him take biology so he can be a farmer). In one episode, they almost came close to getting married. When Dobie and Zelda announced they were getting hitched, Zelda's parents gave their permission, thinking Dobie's parents would never give their consent. Dobie's parents do exactly the same thing. Luckily, the ceremony ground to a halt when Maynard voiced his objection.

Zelda's prediction eventually did come true. In a 1977 pilot for a sequel to the series titled *Whatever Happened to Dobie Gillis?*, Dobie and Zelda are married and have a sixteen-year-old son named Georgie. The unsold pilot was followed by a 1988 two hour made-for-TV movie, *Bring Me the Head of Dobie Gillis,* which concentrates on Georgie Gillis' adventures in high school.

Did You Know?

Zelda's intelligence apparently rubbed off on actress Sheila James Kuehl, who graduated from Harvard Law School and went on to become a prominent and highly respected (and the first openly lesbian) member of the California state legislature.

In his pre-Opie days, Ronny Howard made frequent appearances on the series as a little boy who lived in the Gillis' neighborhood.

The series' title seemed to change as often as Dobie changed girlfriends. The series premiered in 1959 as *The Many Loves of Dobie Gillis,* and was then shortened to *Dobie Gillis* during its second season (1960–61), and then changed again to *Max Shulman's Dobie Gillis* during its final two years (1960–62).

No one knows the exact location of Central City, but you can find one in Colorado, Illinois, Iowa, Kentucky, Nebraska, and Pennsylvania.

RECOMMENDED VIEWING

To get a feel for life in Central City, the following episodes are recommended:

"Dobie's Birthday Party"
Writer: Ed James
Director: Rod Amateau

Dobie tells everyone to forget about his birthday, but he becomes depressed when he thinks everyone has. *Highlight: Dobie and Maynard visit Riff's Record Shop.* Original airdate: 9/1/59

"The Best Dressed Man"
Writer: Max Shulman
Director: Rod Amateau

In order to impress Thalia, Dobie competes with rich kid Milton Armitage's stylish wardrobe by borrowing a new outfit every day from Ralph T. Ziegler's Men's Clothing Store. *Note: Mel Blanc, the voice of Bugs Bunny and dozens of other cartoon characters, plays the clothing shop owner.* Original airdate: 9/22/59

"Lassie, Get Lost"
Writer: Dean Reisner
Director: Rod Amateau

When sex symbol Valentine Van Loan's dog Boo Boo is lost, everyone, especially Dobie, tries to find the pooch to collect the hefty reward. Original airdate: 3/7/63

The Many Loves of Dobie Gillis

Premiere Date: September 29, 1959
CBS   147 episodes

Cast

Dobie Gillis . . . . Dwayne Hickman	Zelda Gilroy . . . . Sheila James
Maynard G. Krebs . . . . Bob Denver	Thalia Menninger.	
Herbert T. Gillis . . . . Frank Faylen	. . . Tuesday Weld (1959–60, 1962)	
Winnie Gillis. . . . . Florida Friebus	Milton Armitage . . . . . Warren Beatty (1959–60)	

Cicely, Alaska

Northern Exposure (1990–95)

Created by Joshua Brand and John Falsey

The fictional town of Cicely, Alaska, is the setting of one of the most original television series of the 1990s. In the pilot episode, Dr. Joel Fleischman, fresh out of medical school, arrives in Anchorage to fulfill his four-year service to the state of Alaska in exchange for his $125,000 medical scholarship. Unfortunately, the hospital in Anchorage is overstaffed, so he is sent to Cicely. On his arrival, Joel is less than pleased with the size of the rural town and its eccentric citizens. For the next four years, the native New Yorker and the only Jew in Arrowhead County has difficulty adapting to living—as he would put it—in the middle of nowhere.

The real star of *Northern Exposure* is the small community of Cicely. The town is a cross-section of American society, where people from different ethnic, cultural, and economic backgrounds peacefully co-exist. The idiosyncrasies of its quirky citizens and the local customs, myths, and superstitions are accepted without question by everyone—except Dr. Fleischman.

Cicely serves as a haven for several characters who have made the town their permanent home: Maggie O'Connell, a feminist bush pilot who moved to Cicely to escape her upper-class family; Chris Stevens,

---

Cicely at a Glance

Where to Stay:
Sourdough Inn Bed & Breakfast $$

Where to Dine:
The Brick (try a Mooseburger!) $

Where to Shop:
Ruth-Anne's General Store

Local Media:
KBHR 570-AM

Local Newspaper:
The Cicely News and World Telegram

When they are not arguing, Dr. Joel Fleischman (Rob Morrow) and Maggie O'Connell (Janine Turner) are keeping each other warm.

The home of Cicely's most famous citizen, ex-astronaut Maurice Minnifield.

the town philosopher who arrived in Cicely after jumping bail in 1986; Ruth-Anne Miller, a widow and the proprietor of the general store who relocated to Cicely from Portland in 1971; and Maurice Minnifield, an ex-astronaut and heir to a $68 million family fortune.

Maurice is responsible for bringing Joel ("a Jew doctor," as he refers to him) to Cicely. With an ego as big as his bank account, Mau-rice is single-handedly trying to transform Cicely into a tourist spot. He owns fifteen thousand acres of land filled with "wildlife just waiting to be fondled." As owner of Minnifield Communications Network, he also controls the town's radio station KBHR (K-Bear 570 AM), and newspaper, *The Cicely News and World Telegram.* Chris is the star DJ at KBHR. His show "Chris in the Morning" provides Cicely residents with local news, bits of wisdom, and some tunes from Maurice's private record collection.

Maurice once tried to boost the readership of the *Cicely News* by allowing Adam, Cicely's resident pathological liar and paranoid (he thinks the FBI is monitoring everyone), to contribute stories to the paper. His piece on talking trees in Alaska increases the paper's readership and creates friction between believers and skeptics like Joel. The story turned out to have some validity due to a chemical spill that actually caused the trees to make crying sounds. Maurice also serves as the town's mayor and always ran unopposed until Edna Hancock decided to throw her hat in the ring. Edna was upset that Maurice never put in the stop sign she requested. She proved to be a worthy opponent and beat Maurice by eight votes (255 to 247). Maggie would later succeed Edna as mayor.

The center of Cicely is the local restaurant/bar, The Brick, which is owned and operated by Holling Vincoeur, an ex-trapper and hunter, and his much younger girlfriend, Shelly Tambo, a former Miss Northwest Passage. Shelly arrived in Cicely as Maurice's fiancée, but fell in love with Holling, which created a short-lived feud between the two friends. Another establishment in Cicely is the Sourdough Inn Bed & Breakfast, owned by two gay ex-marines, Ron Bantz and Erick Hillman. Ron and Erick were immediately accepted by everyone in the town, except for homophobic Maurice, who became very nervous upon discovering he shared their love of cooking

Did You Know?

Where exactly in Alaska is Cicely? The exact location is never given, though some information, at times contradictory, is given throughout the series. Some of these hints include:

- Cicely rests on the 68th parallel, which would place it in the center of the state.

- Cicely is 40 air-miles from Anchorage, yet it's 400 miles from Solodonta, which is approximately 145 miles south of Anchorage.

- Cicely is connected to Cantwell by Route 8 and Highway 1 is close to town. The two roads are actually 75 miles apart.

According to the publicity still for the pilot, the population of Cicely is 215 and the elevation is 6,572 feet. In later episodes, the population is reported to be 849.

and show tunes. But in the spring of 1994, the couple exchanged vows with all of Cicely, including Maurice, in attendance.

The population of Cicely increased by one when lawyer Mike Monroe moved to town. Mike was hyper-allergic to the environment and forced to live in a domed "bubble" house, located off of Highway 3. Maggie had a major crush on Mike, who was cured during his stay in Cicely. He left town soon afterward to continue his fight to save the environment by becoming a lawyer for Greenpeace.

Also included among the townspeople are television's first regular Native American characters: Ed Chigliak, a half-native Alaskan with a high IQ and a passion for film, and Marilyn Whirlwind, Joel's stone-faced secretary, who raises ostriches. The culture and traditions of Native Americans living in the region are predominant in Cicely. Among the holidays celebrated are the annual Indian Day of the Dead Parade at Thanksgiving, the Pageant of the Raven at Christmas, and the Running of the Bulls, which marks the arrival of spring by having all of Cicely's male citizens run naked through the center of town. The change of seasons also has a bizarre effect on the collective consciousness of Cicely's citizens, who have uncontrollable libidos as winter turns to spring and inexplicably appear in each other's dreams when there is a glitch in the Northern Lights.

The founding of Cicely was the subject of a critically-acclaimed episode. According to the legend, a lesbian couple, the strong-willed Roslyn and her sweet, beautiful companion Cicely, arrived in town in 1909. Cicely brought art and culture to the community by opening a salon where the townspeople learn to appreciate poetry and dance. Roslyn attempted to bring order and justice to the lawless town by challenging the evil Mace Mobrey. During a confrontation with

Mace, a gunman shot Roslyn. Cicely intercepted the bullet and died in her lover's arms. The tragedy ironically brought peace to the community, which was thus named Cicely in her honor.

Joel's stay in Cicely ended with a search for the mythical Keewa Ani, the Jeweled City

---

Cicely, Alaska, in Roslyn, Washington

The Roslyn Café
201 W. Pennsylvania Avenue
(509) 649-2763
The mural on the side of this eatery, located in the center of town, can be seen in the opening sequence of the series.

The Brick Tavern
100 W. Pennsylvania Avenue
(509) 649-2643
The exterior of this tavern was used on the series for Holling's place. Founded in 1889, it's one of the oldest taverns in the state of Washington.

Other locations used in the series include Roslyn Realty (112 W. Pennsylvania), which stood in as the exteriors of Joel's office, and Central Sundries (101 W. Pennsylvania Place), which was used for Ruth-Anne's General Store (and now sells *Northern Exposure* memorabilia).

The Brick, famous for its Mooseburger, is the best place to soak up some local color.

of the North. Accompanied by Maggie, he reaches the goal of his quest, only to discover that Keewa Ani is his own hometown—New York City. Maggie bids her friend a final farewell. Meanwhile, Joel's replacement is Dr. Philip Capra, who relocated to Alaska from Los Angeles with his wife Michelle, a freelance journalist. Phil had difficulty adjusting to local customs, while Michelle brought some culture to the town by directing a production of William Inge's *Bus Stop* starring Maggie and Chris.

41

The history behind the real setting of Cicely, Alaska, is equally fascinating. The exteriors of the show were shot on the streets of Roslyn, Washington, a small town (population approximately 800) eighty miles outside of Seattle (interiors were shot on a soundstage in the Seattle suburb of Redmond). But prior to *Northern Exposure,* Roslyn was experiencing economic hardship and high unemployment because the lumber industry was downsized due to the controversy surrounding the preservation of the spotted owl. The program revitalized the town. Locals were hired as extras and stand-ins and the local police department served as security. When the show's popularity increased, culminating with an Emmy for Best Dramatic Series in 1992, Roslyn became a popular tourist attraction. The city and its citizens also received a citation from the Academy of Television Arts & Sciences in recognition of their contribution to the Emmy-winning production.

RECOMMENDED VIEWING

To get a feel for life in Cicely, the following episodes are recommended:

"Spring Break"
Writer: David Assael
Director: Rob Thompson

Spring is in the air and the citizens of Cicely are acting a little crazy. Maggie is having sexual fantasies, Joel's libido is out of control, Holling is in the mood for a good fight, and Shelly becomes an avid reader of classical literature. There's also a kleptomaniac on the loose. This episode features the annual "Running of the Bulls," in which the men of Cicely run naked down Main Street in the snow. Original airdate: 5/6/91

"Cicely"
Writers: Diane Frolov and
Andrew Schneider
Director: Rob Thompson

The history of Cicely, as told by one of the town's oldest living residents. Guest stars Jo Anderson and Yvonne Suhor play Roslyn and Cicely, the town's founders, who brought law and culture to the uncivilized community. Original airdate: 5/18/92

"I Feel the Earth Move"
Writer: Jed Seidel
Director: Michael Fresco

Love is in the air when the citizens of Cicely are preparing for the wedding of Ron and Erick, owners of the local bed and breakfast. The event creates friction between the couple, who have a fight that sends Erick packing. Maurice saves the day by convincing him not to call off the wedding. Meanwhile, Maggie and Joel are having problems of their own. She is convinced that being around Joel is making her nauseous. Original airdate: 5/2/94

Northern Exposure

Premiere Airdate: July 12, 1990
CBS   110 Episodes

Cast

Dr. Joel Fleischman	Rob Morrow	Ruth-Anne Miller	Peg Phillips
Maggie O'Connell	Janine Turner	Ron Bantz	Doug Ballard
Maurice Minnifield	Barry Corbin	Erick Hillman	Don R. McManus
Chris Stevens	John Corbett	Mike Monroe	Anthony Edwards (1992–93)
Ed Chigliak	Darren E. Burrows	Adam	Adam Arkin (1991–95)
Holling Vincoeur	John Cullum	Eve	Valerie Mahaffey (1991–95)
Shelly Tambo	Cynthia Geary	Dr. Philip Capra	Paul Provenza (1994–95)
Marilyn Whirlwind	Elaine Miles	Michelle Capra	Teri Polo (1994–95)

Seaview Terrace, a mansion in Newport, Rhode Island, was used for the exterior shots of Collinwood, the Collins family estate.

Collinsport, Maine

Dark Shadows (1966–71, 1991)

Created by Dan Curtis

While visitors may want to think twice about setting foot in Cabot Cove—the murder capital of television land—there's another small village in Maine that should be avoided at all costs. This coastal town, located fifty miles from Bangor, is inhabited by ghosts, witches, zombies, werewolves, and a 175-year-old vampire named Barnabas Collins. There is also an eighteenth-century estate known as Collinwood, which is haunted by the ancestors of the current inhabitants (and the town's namesake)—the Collins family.

Collinsport is the setting of *Dark Shadows,* a popular daytime serial that combined elements of a soap opera with a Gothic horror film—sort of an *As the World Turns* meets *Dracula.* Most of the action takes place in and around Collinwood, so our view of the adjacent village, located near Frenchman's Bay in Hancock County, Maine, is limited to the Collinsport Inn and the local pub, the Blue Whale. There is also a train depot, where, in the first episode, Victoria Winters arrives to work as a governess for the Collins family. The town is popular with summer vacationers and serves as a haven for reclusive artists. The major industry is fishing. The matriarch of the Collins family, Elizabeth Collins Stoddard, and her brother Roger are the heads of Collins Enterprises, which includes the Collins Cannery and the largest fishing fleet in the area.

Collinsport at a Glance

Where to Stay:
Collinsport Inn $$

Where to Dine:
Collinsport Inn Restaurant $$

Where to Shop:
Brewster's Department Store

Local Hangout:
The Blue Whale
The Three Gables

Local Newspaper:
The Collinsport Gazette

Barnabas Collins (Jonathan Frid) takes a stroll outside of the Old House.

The Collins family reside in Collinwood, a grand mansion outside of town that was being built in a "flashback" episode (actually Victoria travels back in time via a seance) in 1795 and 1796. The house was a wedding present from Joshua Collins to his son Barnabas and his bride, Josette. (As with most soap operas, there are several continuity problems regarding the history of Collinwood. Elizabeth claims her great-grandfather, Jeremiah, built the house). Adjacent to the mansion is the Old House, where the family lived prior to the building of Collinwood. In the present day (the

1960s), the Old House remained abandoned until Barnabas was freed from his coffin and the vampire decided to fix up the place and move in.

Collinwood is a most unusual house. In the east wing there is a stairway that transports characters back in time. In the west wing there is a room that you can open to observe a "parallel universe." In this alternate world, certain aspects of the Collins family's lives are different because of certain choices they have made. There are also various secret passageways and rooms in both Collinwood and the Old House that provide characters the opportunity to escape or creep up on each other. An unsuspecting visitor may also run into a vampire or a werewolf in the surrounding woods or in the family mausoleum. The ghosts of various dead widows of Collinsport are known to haunt Widow's Hill, from which many characters, past and present, have taken a plunge.

Several locations in New England were used for the exteriors of Collinsport and Collinwood. The Collinsport exteriors, such as the police station, Main Street, and the waterfront, were shot in Essex, Connecticut. The Griswold Inn was used for the Collinsport Inn. The exterior of the Blue Whale (known as the Eagle in flashbacks) is the Black Pearl restaurant in Newport, Rhode Island. Newport is also the home of the exterior of Collinwood, the Carey Mansion, also known as Seaview Terrace. The Spratt Mansion on the Lyndhurst estate in Tarry-

town, New York, was used for the Old House (the mansion burned down in the late 1960s.) The interiors were shot at ABC-TV's Studio 2 on West 67th Street, though it moved early in its run to a new studio on 53rd Street.

In 1991, Barnabas Collins was resurrected when *Dark Shadows* was revived as a prime-time series. While the production values of the original series were low due to a limited budget, the 1991 revival had more elaborate sets, make-up, and special effects. The new version was also gorier and sexier, particularly in terms of the relationship between Barnabas and his victims. Once again, the story begins with the arrival of Victoria Winters to Collinwood, yet unlike the origi-

Seaview Terrace
Ruggles Avenue
The mansion used for the exteriors of Collinwood is a sixty-five room French chateau built in 1928 by Edson Bradley, owner of a whiskey distillery. The most recent owner is Martin Carey, brother of former New York Governor Hugh Carey, who leases the house to Salve Regina College, which uses it for classrooms and a dormitory.

The Black Pearl
America's Cup Avenue
The exterior of this New England restaurant was featured on the show as The Blue Whale.

nal series, Barnabas is introduced in the first episode (in the 1960s version he arrived in episode number 211).

In the series revival, Collinwood received a major facelift. The action was no longer restricted to the foyer and the main drawing room of the house, but took place throughout Collinwood and the Old House. Greystone, a fifty-five-room Tudor mansion owned by the city of Beverly Hills was used for the exteriors of Collinwood as well as some of the interiors (some exteriors were shot at Warner Hollywood studios). There is a stronger sense overall of the grandeur of Collinwood with its massive foyer, complete with a grand staircase, and a stately drawing room filled with paintings and antiques. Greystone also doubled for the exterior and parts of the interior of the Old House as well.

This time around viewers also received a more complete picture of the village of Collinsport. Before she is attacked by Barnabas, Daphne Collins leaves the Blue Whale and walks through a quiet residential neighborhood lined with Victorian-style houses (the scene was actually shot on the Warner Bros. backlot in Burbank). In addition to the Blue Whale, the locals hang out at the Three Gables, a bar right outside of town, where a young crowd drinks and dances to rock music. In the dark parking lot of the bar, Barnabas kills his next two victims. Additional locations include the Collinsport train station, hospital, police station, and courthouse.

NBC canceled the revival of the series after thirteen episodes due to low ratings. The series was actually a fatality of the Gulf War, which pre-empted the airing of the fourth episode, and caused the network's constant rescheduling of the remaining episodes. In spite of a protest by loyal *Dark Shadow* fans around the country, who even picketed NBC's headquarters in Burbank, California, the network did not pick up the show for the 1991–92 season.

Did You Know?

The character of Barnabas Collins was originally scheduled to appear in only five episodes. He became popular with viewers and was soon the show's central character.

Several actors who appeared on the original *Dark Shadows* went on to have successful careers in television, film, and on the stage. The list includes Kate Jackson, Conrad Bain, David Groh, Barnard Hughes, John Karlen, Harvey Keitel, Donna Mckechnie, Marsha Mason, Abe Vigoda, Susan Sullivan, and Elizabeth Wilson.

Thanks to the video release of the series and daily repeats on the Sci-Fi Channel, *Dark Shadows* fandom is alive and well.

Kathryn Leigh Scott, who originated the role of Maggie Evans, started her own company, Pomegranate Press, which has published several books about *Dark Shadows*.

Collinsport's most infamous vampire, Barnabas Collins (Jonathan Frid).

Recommended Viewing

Thanks to the miracle of modern technology, 1,225 episodes of the original *Dark Shadows* were released by MPI Video.

The pre-Barnabas episodes are available on the fifty-four–volume "Dark Shadows Collectors Series."

The remainder of the series ("the Barnabas episodes") is available in 200 volumes.

To get a feel for Collinwood and Collinsport from the eighteenth through the twentieth centuries, the following four volumes of the "Barnabas episodes" are recommended:

Volume #1—The Resurrection of Barnabas Collins

This tape contains the highlights of the pre-Barnabas episodes, beginning with the arrival of Victoria Winters through the unleashing of Barnabas by Willie Loomis from his Collins Mausoleum coffin.

Volume #2

Barnabas arrives in Collinsport and meets the Collins family and Maggie Evans, who resembles his late wife, Josette.

Volume #92

The ghost of Quentin Collins has seized control of young David Collins and Amy Jennings. While Professor Stokes attempts to exorcise the ghost from the Collinwood, the Collins family is forced to move into the Old House with Barnabas.

Volume #148

Barnabas enters the mysterious room in Collinwood Mansion and is transported to a parallel time.

Dark Shadows

Premiere Airdate: June 27, 1966
ABC   1,245 Episodes

Cast

Barnabas Collins	Jonathan Frid	Dr. Julia Collins	Grayson Hall
Victoria Winters	Alexandra Moltke	Quentin Collins	David Selby
Elizabeth Collins Stoddard	Joan Bennett	Maggie Evans	Kathryn Leigh Scott
Roger Collins	Louis Edmonds	Carolyn Stoddard	Nancy Barrett
David Collins	David Henesy	Angelique Bourchard	Lara Parker

Dark Shadows (1991 Revival)

Premiere Airdate: January 13, 1991
NBC   13 Episodes

Cast

Barnabas Collins	Ben Cross	Dr. Julia Hoffman	Barbara Steele
Victoria Winters	Joanna Going	Willie Loomis	Jim Fyfe
Elizabeth Collins Stoddard	Jean Simmons	Maggie Evans	Ely Pouget
Roger Collins	Roy Thinnes	Carolyn Stoddard	Barbara Blackburn
David Collins	Joseph Gordon-Levitt		

Fernwood's favorite dysfunctional family. Front row: Heather Hartman (Claudia Lamb), George Shumway (Philip Bruns), Cathy Shumway (Debralee Scott). Back row: Tom Hartman (Greg Mullavey), Martha Shumway (Dody Goodman), Mary Hartman (Louise Lasser), and Grandpa Larkin (Victor Kilian).

Fernwood, Ohio

Mary Hartman, Mary Hartman (1976–77)
Forever Fernwood (1977)

Created by Gail Parent, Ann Marcus, Jerry Adelman, & Daniel Gregory Browne
Developed by Norman Lear

Fernwood 2-Night (1977–78)

Created by Norman Lear

Fernwood, Ohio, is a typical American town, but there is nothing typical about *Mary Hartman, Mary Hartman*. This send-up of daytime soap operas was too off-beat and controversial for network television, though it found an audience in syndication (in a late-night time slot) on independent stations. Mary Hartman is a housewife whose life is a daily struggle thanks to an impotent husband, a grandfather who runs around in a raincoat flashing strangers, an oversexed sister, and yellow waxy buildup on her kitchen floor. Her knowledge of the world is limited to household products, television commercials, and *Reader's Digest*. She is also very bored, yet there's nothing boring about life in Fernwood.

The Hartmans reside at 343 Bratner Avenue in the Woodland Hills section of Fernwood, Ohio. Mary's husband Tom, her father George, and the Hartmans' neighbor Charlie Haggers work on the assembly line at the local automobile plant. Mary raises her teenage daughter Heather, cleans the house, watches TV, and talks on the phone

---

Fernwood at a Glance

Where to Stay:
 The Bide-A-Wee Motel $

Where to Dine:
 The House of Pancakes $
 Denny's $

Nightlife:
 Capri Lounge
 Rosemont Bowling Alley

Where to Shop:
 Safeway
 Federated

Local Newspaper:
 The Fernwood Courier

Fernwood 2-Night's host Barth Gimble (Martin Mull) and sidekick Jerry Hubbard (Fred Willard) chat with singer Tom Waits and "Bud" Prize (played by Kenneth Mars), who discusses the lack of tourism in Fernwood.

to her mother Martha, who lives down the street at 4309 Bratner Avenue.

Like the settings of most soap operas, Fernwood is, on the surface, an ordinary suburban community, yet it is continuously rocked by tragedy and scandal. The Hartmans' neighbors, the Lombardi family—Buck, his wife, their three kids and their two goats and eight chickens—were butchered by a madman (Mary's response: "What kind of madman would shoot two goats and eight chickens?"). The mayor of Fernwood, Merle Jeeter, is a scoundrel who gets caught with a prostitute and hires an ex-con to run the police department. The town attempts to run him out of office, but he manages to turn public opinion by standing naked in front of his constituency and confessing his sins. Jeeter's

eight-year-old son, Jimmy Joe, poses as a child preacher for his father's money-making housing scam, "Condos for Christ." In an ironic twist, the little televangelist is electrocuted when a television falls into his bathtub.

Mary's best friend and neighbor, Loretta Haggers, a born-again Christian, maintains her faith in the Lord as she suffers a series of misfortunes that never dampen her spirits or aspirations to be a country singer. She performs regularly at the Capri Lounge at the Rosemont Bowling Alley, where her repertoire includes a tribute to Patsy Cline. She and husband Charlie lose their home, and she is temporarily paralyzed on her way to Nashville when her car collides with a station wagon full of nuns. Loretta and Charlie are delighted to learn that they're pregnant, only to discover it's actually a huge tumor. When she gets her big breaks and sings on *The Dinah Shore Show*, she casually mentions on-air how helpful her Jewish agents and promoters have been. "I can't believe those are the same people who killed the Lord," she innocently states. Loretta apologizes for her anti-Semitic remark, but her career comes to a standstill.

In addition to keeping her floors shiny, Mary has plenty on her plate. Tom is impotent and has lost sexual interest in her. Grandfather Larkin is arrested for exposing himself and is revealed to be the infamous Fernwood Flasher. When Mary brings chicken soup to the local basketball coach, who has been swigging Jack Daniels and popping pills all day, the coach falls in the soup and drowns. Trying to save her daughter from a mass-murderer, Mary is taken hostage in a Chinese laundry. She accidentally knocks out Sergeant Dennis Foley, her future lover, when he attempts to rescue her.

Although Mary generally appears calm during a crisis, in part because she seems somewhat catatonic most of the time, she finally snaps at the end of the first season. During an appearance as a typical American consumer-housewife on *The David Susskind Show*, Mary has a nervous breakdown. She is committed to the Fernwood Psychiatric Hospital, which is pleased to be taking care of her because they have never had a patient with Mary Hartman's notoriety. Wanda Jeeter, the mayor's wife, commends Mary for making BD's (breakdowns) respectable by having one on television. Mary has trouble adjusting to life in a mental hospital, but she is delighted to discover that the patients' communal television set has a telemeter,

Did You Know?

Mary Hartman, Mary Hartman was rejected by NBC, CBS, and ABC because it was considered too controversial. After its run in syndication, the series eventually made it to network TV when CBS reran the series in a late-night time slot.

Louise Lasser was arrested by a Beverly Hills policeman when she tried to buy an antique dollhouse. When her credit card was denied, Lasser got upset. She was charged with disturbing the peace, cocaine possession, and two unpaid traffic tickets. In a case of art imitating reality, the writers used the same situation when Mary Hartman travels to New York City to appear on *The Susskind Show*.

Mary Kay Place, who won an Emmy for her portrayal of Loretta Haggers, released an album during the series run entitled "Tonight! At the Capri Lounge…Loretta Haggers." Her hit single, "Baby Boy," reached No. 3 on the country music charts and the album was nominated for a Grammy Award.

The voice you hear in the opening sequence shouting "Mary Hartman! Mary Hartman!" belongs to Mary's mother, Martha Shumway, played by Dody Goodman.

making everyone in the psychiatric ward a member of a Nielsen ratings family.

At the end of the second season, Louise Lasser decided to quit the show. In her last episode, Mary Hartman, who has run away with Sergeant Foley, is seen standing with him in her new kitchen commenting on the waxy build-up on her floor. The show continued without Mary Hartman for six more months under the title *Forever Fernwood*. The focus shifted to Tom Hartman and other members of the Fernwood community.

When his soap opera satire ran out of steam, producer Norman Lear turned his attention to the talk show genre. Broadcast from WZAZ-TV, Channel 6 (on Acacia Street) in Fernwood, Ohio, *Fernwood 2-Night* poked fun at local late-night talk shows. The week-night show was hosted by Barth Gimble, whose wife-beating twin brother Garth was impaled by an aluminum Christmas tree on *Mary Hartman*. The egotistical Barth had hosted a talk show back in Miami, where he was being investigated on felony charges. Filling the seat next to him was sidekick Jerry Hubbard, whose brother Conrad was the station manager. Jerry had previously hosted the senior citizen quiz show on WZAZ-TV, *Dialing for Dentures*. Happy Kyne and the Mirth Makers supplied the music. Happy never smiled, but he was always eager to promote his fast-food restaurant, Bun 'n' Run.

The guests who appeared on the premiere episode of *Fernwood 2-Night* set the tone for the remainder of the series: Howard Palmer, who played Mozart on the piano while lying in his iron lung; Morton Rose, who was passing

Did You Know?

Fernwood 2-Night was produced by Alan Thicke, who would later go on to host his own short-lived talk show, *Thicke of the Night,* and star as Dr. Jason Seaver on the sitcom *Growing Pains.* Robin Williams and Paul Reubens, who would later become known as Pee-Wee Herman, also made appearances on the show.

through town and was asked to appear on the show because most Fernwood residents had never seen a "real live" Jew; and Dr. Osgood, who presented his theory that leisure suits cause cancer. The show also featured representatives from local organizations, including members of the Fernwood All-State Women's Basketball Team, the Fernwood Fascinating Females League, and the Fernwood Gun Association presenting their Kiddie Krime Korps program, which would give guns to young children as a means of fighting crime. Regular segments included "Bury the Hatchet," which allowed two people on opposite sides of an issue to talk it out, and "Rocket to Stardom," which showcased local talent. Two up-and-comers featured were little Baby Irene, who sang "I Didn't Know the Gun was Loaded," and Darryl Washington, an African-American boy (who was bused in from Cincinnati) to do a disco hula-hoop number.

One year later, *Fernwood 2-Night* went national when Barth and Jerry moved their talk show to Alta Coma, California—the unfinished furniture capital of the world. Retitled *America-2 Night*, the series retained its bizarre sense of humor. Taking advantage of its West Coast location, it also featured (in a format that would be repeated fourteen years later on *The Larry Sanders Show*) actual celebrities playing themselves, including Charleton Heston, Elke Sommer, and Carol Burnett.

RECOMMENDED VIEWING

The Best of Mary Hartman, Mary Hartman, Volumes 1 and 2.

Highlights of the series can be seen on a two volume tape set (currently out of print) which includes the first and last episodes of the series.

Mary Hartman, Mary Hartman/ Forever Fernwood

Premiere Airdate: January 1976
Syndicated   325 Episodes

Cast

Mary Hartman . . . . Louise Lasser (1976–77)	Charlie Haggers . . . . Graham Jarvis
Tom Hartman . . . . Greg Mullavey	Merle Jeeter . . . . Dabney Coleman
Martha Shumway . . . . Dody Goodman	Wanda Jeeter . . . . Marian Mercer
George Shumway . . . . . . Philip Bruns (1976–77)	Garth Gimble . . . . Martin Mull (1976–77)
George Shumway . . . . Tab Hunter (1976–77)	Pat Gimble . . . . Susan Browning (1976–77)
Cathy Shumway . . . . Debralee Scott	Eleanor Major . . . . Shelly Fabares (1977–78)
Heather Hartman . . . . Claudia Lamb	Mac Slattery . . . . Dennis Burkley (1977–78)
Raymond Larkin . . . . Victor Kilian	Penny Major . . . . Judy Kahan (1977–78)
Loretta Haggers . . . . Mary Kay Place	Harmon Farinella . . . . . Richard Hatch (1977–78)

Fernwood 2-Night/America 2-Night

Premiere Airdate: July 1977
Syndicated   125 Episodes

Cast

Barth Gimble . . . . Martin Mull	Happy Kyne . . . . Frank DeVol
Jerry Hubbard . . . . Fred Willard	

Gilligan's Island

Gilligan's Island (1964–67)

Created by Sherwood Schwartz

When the SS *Minnow* set sail one day from a tropic port for a three-hour tour (which includes a free lunch), no one could have predicted what was in store for the ship's two crew members and five passengers. The weather suddenly started getting rough, the tiny ship was tossed. If it were not for the courage of its fearless crew, the Minnow would be lost. The ship landed on the shore of an uncharted desert island. Realizing that they might be there indefinitely, they built shelter and found food and fresh water. In spite of having no phones, no lights, no motorcar—not a single luxury, they do their very best to make themselves comfortable in their tropical island nest.

The seven castaways who reside on Gilligan's Island, located approximately three hundred miles southeast of Honolulu, have very diverse backgrounds and interests. Jonas Gumby, the captain of the SS *Minnow* and fondly known as "The Skipper," is an ex-navy man who served in the South Pacific. His first mate, Willie Gilligan, saved his life by stopping a depth charge from rolling down a ship's deck toward him. The Skipper loves Gilligan, who he affectionately refers to as "Little Buddy," but also

---

Gilligan's Island at a Glance

Where to Stay:
   The supply hut $0

Where to Dine:
   The picnic table $0

Nightlife:
   The picnic table

The castaways never lose hope they will be rescued. From the top clockwise: Ginger Grant (Tina Louise), Mrs. Howell (Natalie Schafer), Thurston Howell III (Jim Backus), Gilligan (Bob Denver), The Professor (Russell Johnson), The Skipper (Alan Hale, Jr.) and Mary Ann (Dawn Wells).

finds him a constant source of frustration because everything Gilligan touches turns into a disaster.

Among the passengers are Mr. Thurston Howell, III, and his wife, Eunice "Lovey" Wentworth Howell; Ginger Grant; Professor Roy Hinkley; and Mary Ann Summers. Originally from Grosse Pointe, Michigan, the Howells are the millionaire owners of Howell Industries. Although they were only going on a three-hour tour, the Howells brought along several hundred thousand dollars in cash and an extensive wardrobe. Adding a touch of beauty to the island is Ginger Grant, a "B" movie star whose career was on the rise before getting shipwrecked (she was set to star on Broadway in a play written for her). Ginger has a long list of film credits, which include *Belly Dancers From Bali, The Bird People Meet the Chicken Pluckers*, and *Sing a Song of Sing Sing*. Rounding out the list of island residents are Mary Ann Summers, a farm girl from Winfield, Kansas, and Professor Roy Hinkley, a high school teacher. The multilingual Professor, who was in the middle of writing a book called *Fun With Ferns*, is a wealth of information and is able create even the most complex device out of some bamboo and twine.

The weather on the tropical island is typically warm and sunny, though the castaways often have to deal with bad weather and natural disasters. They have braved tropical storms, a typhoon, and a near volcano eruption. At one point, the castaways thought the island was sinking, only to discover that Gilli-

gan had been moving the stick the Professor was using to measure the water level. A meteor once landed on the island, and they were afraid it was giving off rays that were speeding up their aging process. Luckily, it was destroyed by lightning.

The portion of the island on which the castaways settled has a fairly simple layout. There are four huts which are divided among the castaways. The first, which contains two "bunk hammocks," belongs to Gilligan and the Skipper. French doors give Mr. and Mrs. Howell's hut an added touch of elegance. Ginger and Mary Ann's hut comes complete with a make-up table and a closet to hang Ginger's dresses. The Professor's hut includes a table that he uses to work on his latest invention. A fifth hut is used for supplies. At the center of the huts is a picnic table, where the castaways enjoy their meals (which consist mostly of coconuts, bananas, and fish), hold meetings, and pass the time. The castaways' little village is close to a lagoon, where boats visiting the island usually land. The island also contains a dormant volcano, several caves, and cliffs that overlook the ocean.

The castaways' only source of entertainment, and their only connection to civilization, is a white radio, which they used to listen to music and news reports. Sometimes the news they hear is not so good: Mr. Howell learns that he lost his fortune (it turns out to be a mistake); the Skipper learns that the Maritime Board of Inquiry found him guilty of negligence (their decision is re-

Life on the island is never dull for the Skipper (Alan Hale, Jr.) as long as
Gilligan (Bob Denver) is around.

versed when the storm is determined to be the cause); Gilligan discovers that he has a winning sweepstakes ticket (but he can't find it); and Mary Ann's boyfriend has married someone else (but he wasn't really her boyfriend).

To pass the time, the castaways are forced to entertain themselves. They build a small outdoor theater, which is used for their musical version of *Hamlet* and Mr. Howell's production of *Pyramid for Two*, starring Lovey as Cleopatra. When Mrs. Howell realizes Ginger is upset about not playing the lead, she pretends to have laryngitis and lets Ginger go on in her place. Mrs. Howell also organized a symphony orchestra, whose playing unfortunately was misinterpreted by the natives living on a nearby island as a declaration of war. When a movie company's equipment washes up on shore, the castaways use it to make a silent film reenacting their shipwreck on the island. The completed film is found, but no one seems to interpret it as a cry for help (although it does win an award at the Cannes Film Festival). For something a little less lowbrow, there are turtle races and a "Miss Deserted Island" Beauty Pageant, which is won by Gilligan's monkey, Gladys, the only contestant who is an actual native of the island.

They also learn about what's going on back in civilization from the many visitors who arrive on the island, none of whom is willing or able to rescue the castaways. Many of the people who somehow end up on the island are a little lost themselves or on the run or are simply looking for a little peace and quiet. The island is a haven for bankrobber Jackson Farrell (Larry Storch), the rock 'n' roll group the Mosquitos (Bingo, Bango, Bongo, and Irving, played by the Wellingtons, who sing the title song), and a well-known abstract artist Alexandri Gregor Dubov (Harold J. Stone), who left the mainland ten years ago to get away from critics who panned his work. Pancho Hernando Gonzales Enrico Rodriguez (Nehemiah Persoff), the deposed dictator from the Republica Ecuarico in South America, is exiled to the island, which he tries to turn into his new regime ("Ecuarico West"). When there is a counterrevolution back in his country, he returns, only to leave the castaways behind. Wrongway Feldman (Hans Conried), an incompetent pilot who earned his name when he accidentally bombed his own base in the 1930s, has been living on the island because he's afraid to fly again. When he regains his confidence and arrives on the mainland, he can't remember the location of the island. Feldman returns to the island once again to escape the fast-pace and noise of the city. When the castaways try to make the island less peaceful so he'll return home and they can be rescued, he takes off for another island instead. Another visitor who arrived straight out of a time warp is a Japanese sailor (Vito Scotti), who doesn't know World War II has ended (and his side lost). He takes some of the castaways prisoner, but Gilligan and the Skipper manage to rescue them. Unfortunately, they are not able to radio for help from the

Did You Know?

In the original pilot for *Gilligan's Island*, Ginger was a secretary rather than a movie star, traveling with her friend Bunny, who would eventually become Mary Ann in the series. The Professor, Ginger, and Mary Ann were all recast for the series. The opening song for the pilot was a calypso number, which was changed to a song with a more contemporary sound. Some of the footage from the pilot can be see in the first episode.

The pilot was shot in Hawaii, but the production of the series moved to a less tropical location—CBS Studios in Studio City, which is in the San Fernando Valley section of Los Angeles. The lagoon was actually a man-made concrete lake.

Apparently some viewers took the show too seriously and contacted the U.S. Coast Guard to ask why they had not rescued the castaways.

Although *Gilligan's Island* consistently won its time slot, CBS decided to sacrifice the series so they could move *Gunsmoke* into the Monday evening, 7:30–8:30 P.M. time slot.

submarine before the soldier gets away. Two Russian cosmonauts, Igor (Vincent Beck) and Ivan (Danny Klega) also accidentally land on the island and think the castaways are spies. Once again, the visitors are rescued before the castaways can signal home for help.

In addition to the occasional storm and volcano eruption, the island can provide other dangers. A native chief on a nearby island wants Gilligan to marry his unattractive daughter. The evil Dr. Balinkoff uses the castaways for his mind-switching experiments and returns in another episode to turn them into robots. And then there's the big game hunter, Jonathan Kincaid, who decides he wants to hunt humans and chooses Gilligan for his first prey.

Several other visitors seemed to be more likely candidates for rescuing the castaways, socialite Enika Tiffany Smith (Zsa Zsa Gabor) considers building a resort on the island, but when she returns to the mainland, she can't remember the location. The same thing happens to surfer Duke Williams (Denny Scott Miller), who returns to Hawaii on a tsunami but hits his head on his board and loses his memory.

The castaways would have to wait eleven years until they were finally rescued. In the made-for-TV movie, *Rescue From Gilligan's Island*, a tidal wave destroys the island, leaving the castaways drifting in the ocean until they are saved by the Coast Guard. As they try to resume their lives on the mainland, they begin to realize how much the world has changed. When they reunite for a cruise on the *Minnow II,* the ship gets caught in a storm. Once again, the seven friends find themselves back on their island. They return to civilization in a World War II plane the following year in *The Castaways on Gilligan's Island.* They return to the island, where they go to work for the Howells, who have built a resort hotel: Ginger provides the entertainment, Mary Ann runs the exercise program, the Professor gives lectures, and the Skipper and Gilligan provide transportation to and from the island. A third made-for-TV movie, *The Harlem Globetrotters on Gilligan's Island,* involves the plot of a mad billionaire who tries to drive everyone off the island so he can get hold of the island's supply of supremium, a rare element.

RECOMMENDED VIEWING

To get a feel for life on *Gilligan's Island,* the following episodes are recommended:

"President Gilligan"
Writer: Roland Wolpert
Director: Richard Donner

An example of democracy in the making: the castaways decided to hold elections to select the president of the island. The Skipper and Mr. Howell face off in the election, but Gilligan emerges the victor. Original airdate: 10/31/64

"Gilligan Meets Jungle Boy"
Writers: Al Schwartz, Howard Merrill, and Howard Harris
Director: Lawrence Dobkin

A very young Kurt Russell guest-stars as a jungle boy Gilligan finds on the island. He doesn't speak any English, which poses a problem when he sails off the island in the professor's gas balloon. Original airdate: 2/6/65

"Seer Gilligan"
Writer: Elroy Schwartz
Director: Leslie Goodwins

A bush on the island produces berries which give the castaways the ability to read each other's minds. Morale reaches an all time low as everyone finds out what the others really think about them. Original airdate: 1/27/66

Gilligan's Island

Premiere Airdate: September 26, 1964
CBS   98 Episodes

Cast

Willie Gilligan . . . . Bob Denver
Jonas Gumby (The Skipper) . . . . . Alan Hale, Jr.
Thurston Howell III . . . . Jim Backus
Eunice "Lovey" Wentworth Howell
                . . . . Natalie Schafer

Ginger Grant. . . . . Tina Louise
Roy Hinkley (The Professor) . . Russell Johnson
Mary Ann Summers. . . . . Dawn Wells

Gotham City

Batman (1966–68)

Based on characters created by Bob Kane

Produced for television by William Dozier

Gotham City—the home of the Dynamic Duo, Batman and Robin—is a Crime-ridden metropolis. That's Crime with a capital "C" because the criminals who wreak havoc on this fair city are not petty thieves and small town hoods, but supervillains who are greedy for wealth and power. Luckily, Batman and Robin are only a Batphone call away.

Gotham City, whose streets and parks look remarkably like New York City, was founded by three families who landed on Gotham Rock: the Savages, the Tylers, and the ancestors of millionaire Bruce Wayne (a.k.a. Batman). The original land was leased by the Mohican Indians for the price of nine raccoon pelts. According to the city charter, the lease must be renewed every year. The living descendants of the three original families—Bruce Wayne, Peter Savage, and Tim Tyler (owner of Tyler stadium)—must each present three raccoon pelts by a certain day and time to the last of the Mohican Indians, Chief Screaming Chicken. When Egghead ("the rottenest egg of them all!") steals the charter and prevents the three millionaires from making their

---

Gotham City at a Glance

Where to Dine:
   The Penguin's Nest $$$$

Hot Spot:
   What a Way to Go-Go! Discotheque

Local Newspapers:
   Gotham City Times
   Gotham City Herald

Local TV Station:
   KGOM-TV

The Batcave is only a pole ride away for Batman (Adam West) and the Boy Wonder (Burt Ward).

The streets of Gotham City are safe thanks to Batman (Adam West) and Robin (Burt Ward).

pelt payment on time, he buys Gotham City for himself. He fires Mayor Lindseed and takes over the city. Chaos erupts, but Batman manages to get the town back from Egghead on a technicality—the charter explicitly states that a criminal can't lease the land Gotham City was built on.

Millionaire philanthropist Bruce Wayne resides on the outskirts of Gotham City in stately Wayne mansion with his Aunt Harriet and young ward Dick Grayson (a.k.a. Robin, the Boy Wonder). The Wayne family name is on many Gotham City buildings, including Wayne Memorial Clock Tower, which contains a giant bell (Big Benjamin), presented to the city by Bruce in memory of his father. Not much is known about the millionaire's background, except that his parents were murdered by villains. The only one who knows Batman and Robin's true identities is Bruce's loyal butler, Alfred, who offers his assistance in crime-stopping matters and keeps their outfits ready-to-wear at a moment's notice. Batman's cave is located underneath the Wayne mansion—just lift the head on the bust near the telephone in the study and when the bookcase behind you opens, slide down the Batpole into the Batcave. Then it's only a fourteen mile ride in the Batmobile to Gotham City, where Police Commissioner Gordon and Captain O'Hara will give you an update on current criminal activity.

Gotham City attracts so many supervillains because it's filled to the brim with money and treasure. Among the favorite spots criminals have tried to loot are the Gotham Art Museum (the Joker), the First National Bank (Zelda), the Gotham City Museum (King Tut), the Gotham City Mint (Catwoman), the Gotham City Bank (the Riddler, the Joker, Nora Clavicle), and the American, National, Beneficial, Commercial, Diversified, Empire, and Federal State Banks (the Black Widow). On a smaller scale, some of the treasures which have been pilfered include the Circle of Ice diamonds (Mr. Freeze), the Mergenberg Crown (False Face), the Black Angus Cattle (Shame), and the Sword of Bulbul, the Egg of Ogg, and

Did You Know?

A popular running gag on the show involved the appearance of a celebrity or a popular television character at a window that Batman and Robin pass as they climb up a building. Among the actors who appeared were Jerry Lewis, Sammy Davis Jr., Howard Duff, Werner Klemperer (as *Hogan's Heroes*' Colonel Klink), Ted Cassidy (as *The Addams Family*'s Lurch), Steve Allen, Andy Devine (as Santa), Art Linkletter, Edward G. Robinson, and Van Williams and Bruce Lee (as *The Green Hornet and Kato)*, who would later team up with Batman and Robin to stop Colonel Gumm's counterfeiting ring.

After the first season, a feature-length Batman film was produced featuring the Catwoman, the Joker, the Penguin, and the Riddler, who together try to take over the world.

Aunt Harriet did not appear in the original comic book. Her character was written into the series to squelch any suggestion that Bruce Wayne and Dick Grayson were lovers!

When *Batman* was canceled by ABC after three seasons, NBC was interested in picking up the series. Unfortunately, the sets, including the Batcave, were taken down and it would have been too expensive to rebuild them.

fifty pounds of caviar (Egghead and Olga, Queen of the Bessarovian Cossacks).

Some villains have come dangerously close to controlling Gotham City. Mr. Freeze threatened to deep freeze the entire city if he wasn't paid a billion dollars. King Tut placed a giant sphinx in Gotham Central Park and declared himself the ruler of Gotham City. The Penguin took a more legitimate approach and convinced the citizens of Gotham that he had reformed his ways. After donating $100,000 to the Gotham Charity Fund, beating up a thug trying to rob a blind man, and saving a baby, he received an endorsement by the *Gotham City Times* and the Gotham City Newsdealer Association as a candidate for mayor ("Tippecanoe and Pengy Too" was one of his campaign slo-

gans). Knowing he will never be able to defeat the Penguin, Mayor Linseed convinces Batman to run for office. The Caped Crusader does poorly in the polls because he sticks to the issues and is labeled a child hater because he won't kiss babies ("it's not sanitary"). The Penguin even sabotages Batman's speech during a televised debate on WGOM-TV. When Batman still emerges as the victor, the Penguin kidnaps the Board of Elections, but luckily the new mayor is around to save the day (while Batman receives a phone call from an unnamed party to run for president in the '68 election).

When it is not being terrorized by villains, Gotham City actually has lots to offer tourists or anyone who may be just passing through town. Some of the highlights include the What A Way to Go-Go! Discotheque, where Batman has been seen dancing the Batusi while poor Robin, who is underage, has to wait outside. For something a little more cultural, there is Madame Soleil's Wax Museum, the Bioscope Movie Studio, the Gotham City Museum of Modern Art, and the Gotham City Public Library, which boasts a large collection of rare books that someone is always trying to steal.

When a villain comes to town, he or she never seems to have trouble finding a place to set up his or her hideout. There is always an empty warehouse that can be used to open a temporary business to serve as a front for criminal activity. Some of the more memorable companies include the Amalgamated Ice Cream Company (Mr. Freeze); the Gato

Meeoow! The Catwoman (Julie Newmar) keeps the Dynamic Duo on their their toes by wreaking havoc in Gotham City.

(Spanish for "cat") and Chat (French for "cat") Fur Co. (Cat Woman); the Ghoti-Deufs Caviar Co. (Egghead); and the Pink Chip Stamp Co. (Colonel Gumm). In keeping with their individual identities, the villains usually devise elaborate devices to destroy the Dynamic Duo. Mr. Freeze tries to turn them into human snow cones. The Clock King plans to bury them alive in sand in a giant hour glass. The Joker hooks them up to a giant slot machine that will send 50,000 volts through their bodies. Luckily, Batman and Robin are equipped with Super-Thermo-B-Long Underwear or conveniently have devices such as the Bat Blowtorch, the False Inflatable Batmobile, and Batantidotes, to name a few.(Why these villains don't stick around and watch the Dynamic Duo die is a mystery.) The Dynamic Duo received some help in the third season from Batgirl, who is actually Barbara Gordon, the police commissioner's daughter (only Alfred knows Batgirl's true identity). She was introduced in a 1967 episode in which she rides her Batgirlcycle to the Penguin's hideout where she saves Batman and Robin.

RECOMMENDED VIEWING

To get a feel for life in Gotham City, the following episodes are recommended. *Batman* episodes are in two parts. Part One usually concludes with a cliffhanger ending where Batman and Robin's lives are in grave danger. The narrator invites viewers to tune back in at the "same Bat time, same Bat channel" to find out what happens in Part Two.

"Instant Freeze"
"Rats Like Cheese"
Written by: Max Hodge
Director: Robert Butler
Mr. Freeze seeks revenge on the Dynamic Duo by putting them in a deep freeze, and he steals some diamonds from the Gotham City Diamond Exchange in the process. *Note: a very young Teri Garr makes a brief appearance*. Original airdates: January 2 and 3, 1966

"Hi Diddle Riddle"
"Smack in the Middle"
Writer: Lorenzo Semple Jr.
Director: Robert Butler
The Riddler tricks the Dynamic Duo into falsely arresting him in order to sue Batman and force him to reveal his true identity during the trial. Batman and Robin manage to outfox the Riddler and prevent him from stealing the Mammoth of Moldavia (which is filled with priceless Moldavian postage stamps) from the Gotham City World's Fair. Original airdates: January 12 and 13, 1966

"Hizzonner the Penguin"
"Dizzonner the Penguin"
Writer: Stanford Sherman
Director: Oscar Rudolph
The Penguin runs for mayor of Gotham City by engaging in some dirty politics, but Batman manages to win by running an honest campaign. *Note: Paul Revere and the Raiders provide the music at the Penguin's rally.* Original airdates: November 2 and 3, 1966

Batman

Premiere Airdate: January 12, 1966
ABC   120 Episodes

Cast

Batman/Bruce Wayne . . . . Adam West
Robin/Dick Grayson . . . . Burt Ward
Alfred Pennyworth. . . . . Alan Napier
Aunt Harriet Cooper . . . . Madge Blake

Police Commissioner Gordon. . . . Neil Hamilton
Chief O'Hara . . . . Stafford Repp
Barbara Gordon/Batgirl
            . . . . Yvonne Craig (1967–68)

The Villains

The Riddler . . . . Frank Gorshin
            . . . . John Astin (1967)
The Penguin. . . . . Burgess Meredith
The Joker . . . . Cesar Romero
Mr. Freeze. . . . . George Sanders (1966)
            . . . . Otto Preminger (1966)
            . . . . Eli Wallach (1967)
Zelda the Great . . . . Anne Baxter
The Mad Hatter . . . . David Wayne
False Face . . . . Malachi Throne
Catwoman . . . . Julie Newmar (1966)
            . . . . Eartha Kitt (1967–68)
King Tut . . . . Victor Buono
The Bookworm . . . . Roddy McDowell
The Archer . . . . Art Carney
The Minstrel . . . . Van Johnson
Ma Parker . . . . Shelley Winters

The Clock King . . . . Walter Slezak
Egghead . . . . Vincent Price
Chandell . . . . Liberace
Marsha, Queen of Diamonds . . . Carolyn Jones
The Puzzler . . . . Maurice Evans
Nora Clavicle. . . . . Barbara Rush
Colonel Gumm. . . . . Roger C. Carmel
Shame. . . . . Cliff Robertson
The Black Widow . . . . Tallulah Bankhead
The Siren . . . . Joan Collins
Louie the Lilac . . . . Milton Berle
Lord Fogg. . . . . Rudy Vallee
Lady Penelope Peasoup . . . . Glynis Johns
Dr. Cassandra Spellcraft . . . . Ida Lupino
Cabala . . . . Howard Duff
Minerva. . . . . Zsa Zsa Gabor

Hazzard, Georgia

The Dukes of Hazzard (1979–85)

Created by Gy Wadron

Welcome to Hazzard County, Georgia! Once you cross the county line and continue on through into Hazzard, keep your eye out for the General Lee—a '69 orange Dodge Charger with an "01" on the doors and a Confederate flag on the roof. Look quick, because chances are that either Lucas "Luke" Duke or his younger cousin, Beauregard "Bo" Duke, are behind the wheel, which means Sheriff Roscoe P. Coltrane can't be too far behind. The sheriff spends most of his waking hours chasing down the Duke boys, who always manage to get away (but not without doing a little damage first).

Racing cars, running moonshine, and just plain having a good old time are what the good old folks in Hazzard do best. The Duke boys live outside of town with their Uncle Jesse and cousin Daisy, who's tall, sexy, and can throw a mean punch. The Duke family has a long history of moonshining and Uncle Jesse was legendary in the county as a moonshine runner. When they got caught, Uncle Jesse, Luke, and Bo agreed never to make, sell, or transport whiskey again in exchange for their freedom. As part of their probation, Bo and Luke can not carry guns, so they must resort to using an archer's bow and arrow when absolutely necessary. Bo and Luke believe they aren't breaking the law, they are just sort of bending it in their favor. You

---

Hazzard County at a Glance

Where to Stay:
The No Tell Motel $

Where to Dine:
The Boar's Head $

Where to Shop:
Capitol City Department Store

Local Newspaper:
Hazzard County Gazette

Local Media:
WHOGG Radio

Luke (Tom Wopat) and Bo Duke (John Schneider) take an afternoon stroll through the streets of Hazzard County.

wouldn't think so if you read their rap sheet, which includes speeding, reckless driving, and resisting arrest (and that's only the half of it).

One man who is waiting for the day he can put the Duke boys permanently behind bars is county commissioner and the richest man in Hazzard County, Boss Jefferson Davis Hogg. Hogg is literally the boss of Hazzard because he owns most of the county. In addi-

Uncle Jesse Duke (Denver Pyle) needs a little help getting his engine started by (left to right), nephews Bo (John Schneider) and Luke (Tom Wopat) and niece Daisy (Catherine Bach).

tion to being president of the bank, he owns an Atlanta-based record company, a grits mill, and the local real estate company. Most important of all, Hogg has Sheriff Coltrane in his pocket. Coltrane was an honest lawman for thirty years, but when he lost most of his pension when a bond bill was defeated in a local election, he became "the best lawman money can buy." He's also inept when it comes to being Hazzard's chief lawman, es-

pecially when it involves the Duke boys, who have no problem outsmarting (and outracing) the befuddled sheriff. The same goes for the gullible Officer Straitt who is basically a good guy (he has the hots for Daisy), but not much of a policeman.

Driving through town in his chauffeur-driven white Cadillac Coupe de Ville, Boss Hogg has an ego as big as his bank account. He even went so far as to buy a tank to turn it into a war memorial for himself and "less important heroic veterans of Hazzard County." He and his wife Lulu, who is Roscoe's older sister, have also been immortalized as the namesakes of several county traditions, including: the Lulu Hogg Stakes Horse Race at the County Fair; Sadie Hogg Day, in which a women take over government jobs for the day; and a new event—the J. D. Hogg Hazzard Derby, at which he gets every car that loses or doesn't make it over the finish line.

Hogg also owns the local hangout, the Boar's Nest, which charges a one-dollar cover to keep out the riff-raff. The Nest boasts the "World's Best Tastin' Bar-b-que" and a jukebox just perfect for juking, which is a combination of "music, exercise, and social intercourse on a high plane." On occasion, the Boar's Nests hosts some live talent, which has included performances by Loretta Lynn and Mel Tillis.

Boss Hogg is as crooked as they come and would think nothing of confiscating illegal property and turning it around to sell at a profit. He would even stoop so low as to close down an orphanage to build a new shopping center. With Roscoe's help, he is always trying to pin something on the Dukes or repossess their farm. When he's not dealing with Luke and Bo, he's usually contending with his nephew Hughie, who drops into Hazzard County to make some trouble. Hughie not only follows in his uncle's footsteps by trying to frame the Dukes for moonshining, but he goes after his own uncle, trying to cheat him out of property or blackmail him into mak-

Did You Know?

The first few episodes of *Dukes of Hazzard* were shot in and around Covington, Georgia, located thirty-four miles east of Atlanta. The same town was transformed into Sparta, Mississippi, for the TV series *In the Heat of the Night*. The Dukes were then moved to the backlot of Warner Bros. Studios in Burbank. The backroad chases were shot at the Walt Disney Ranch in Lake Sherwood, California, (twenty miles north of Los Angeles) and Valencia, California.

While there is no Hazzard County in Georgia, there is a Hazard, Kentucky (there's only one "z" in this Hazard). Located forty miles from Lexington, Hazard is a coal-mining town that enjoyed a rise in tourism because of its connection, if only in name, with the series. Several cast members have visited the town. When several residents were killed in a mining accident, Wopat and Schneider did a benefit concert for the victims' families.

Hazzard police officer Enos Straitt, who was a little short-changed in the brains department, was spun off into his own series. The short-lived *Enos* was set in Los Angeles, where Enos worked for the Los Angeles Police Department. When the show was canceled, Enos returned to his old job in Hazzard County.

ing Hughie sheriff. Ironically, it's the Duke boys who come to Hogg's rescue.

Criminals seem to be drawn to Hazzard County. Over the years they've been visited by mobsters, counterfeiters, con men, car strippers, hijackers, and an visitor from outer space, who, like ET, the Dukes help get safely home.

While Bo and Luke were off driving on the NASCAR (National Association of Stock Car Auto Racing) circuit, Uncle Jesse received two visitors. Nephews Coy and Vance Duke arrived in town and picked up where their cousins left off by driving fast and interfering in Boss Hogg's business every chance they could get. The temporary change is an interesting chapter in Hazzard's history. The absence of stars Tom Wopat and John Schneider during the beginning of the fifth

season was due to contractual problems between the actors and the producers of the series, Warner Bros. Studios. They filed a $25 million lawsuit against the studio for failing to pay them revenue from *Dukes'* merchandising. The studio, in turn, sued them for not reporting to work. Eventually, the lawsuits were dropped and a settlement for an undisclosed amount was paid. When Bo and Luke returned to Hazzard, Coy and Vance stuck around just long enough for a handshake goodbye and off they went, never to return.

Hazzard County holds several annual celebrations. Most have to do with cars, such as the Obstacle Race, in which drivers participate in a free-for-all to get to the finish line, and the Hazzard "Drag-in-Fly" Derby, a combination race and car jumping contest. The Ridgerunners Association, a group of old time moonshine runners that includes Uncle Jesse and Boss Hogg, sponsors a get-together and a race. A celebration is also held to commemorate Stonewall Jackson Day. Hogg even brought Jackson's sword used during the Civil War to Hazzard, but only so he could steal it and sell it for the cash.

A two-hour made-for-TV movie, *The Dukes of Hazzard: Reunion!* brought Bo, Luke, and Daisy back to Hazzard for the Homecoming Festival. In an effort to stop Sheriff Roscoe and his new partner in crime, Mama Max, from building a theme park in Hazzard, they are forced to enter the General Lee in a race. Once again, the Duke Boys are victorious! A second Dukes reunion premiered in May 2000.

Did You Know?

Over three hundred Dodge Chargers were destroyed during the series' run.

After the series, Ben Jones, who played garage mechanic Cooter Davenport, pursued a political career. He was elected for two terms (1988 and 1990) to the House of Representatives (D–Georgia, 4th district), a district that included Covington, Georgia. Jones lost his seat when the district was reapportioned in 1992. He tried again in 1994, but lost to Newt Gingrich.

Recommended Viewing

To get a feel for life in Hazzard County, Georgia, the following episodes are recommended viewing:

"One-Armed Bandits"
Writer: Gy Waldron
Director: Rod Amateau

In the debut episode, Bo and Luke hijack a shipment of slot machines from Boss Hogg and help save a local orphanage with the profits. Original airdate: 1/26/79

"Mrs. Daisy Hogg"
Writer: Si Rose
Director: John Florea

Everyone's worst nightmare is about to come true: Boss Hogg's nephew Jamie Lee has proposed to Daisy Duke. In order to prevent their cousin from becoming a Hogg, Duke and Bo have to expose Jamie Lee as a counterfeiter. Original airdate: 10/9/81

"Nothin' but the Truth"
Writer: Martin Roth
Director: Hollingsworth Morse

Boss Hogg plants gambling machines on the Dukes in order to divert attention from his own illegal casino operation. When Hogg is accidentally poked with a syringe full of truth serum, he begins to reveal every illegal act he's ever committed. Once again, the Dukes have to rescue Hogg when he is kidnapped by his partners in the casino operation, who are afraid he'll tell too much. Original airdate: 2/5/82

Dukes of Hazzard

Premiere Airdate: January 26, 1979
CBS   145 Episodes

Cast

Luke Duke . . . . Tom Wopat	Deputy Enos Straitt	
Bo Duke . . . . John Schneider	Sonny Shroyer (1979–80, 1982–85)	
Daisy Duke . . . . Catherine Bach	Cooter . . . . Ben Jones	
Uncle Jesse Duke . . . . Denver Pyle	Coy Duke . . . . Byron Cherry (1982–83)	
Sheriff Roscoe P. Coltrane . . . . James Best	Vance Duke . . . . . Christopher Mayer (1982–83)	
Jefferson Davis "Boss" Hogg . . . Sorrell Booke		

When you see the water tower, you will know you've arrived at the junction . . . Petticoat Junction.

Hooterville

Petticoat Junction (1963–70)
Created by Paul Henning

Green Acres (1965–71)
Created by Jay Sommers

Hooterville (or as Lisa Douglas pronounces it, "Hooters-ville") was the setting for two popular rural sitcoms of the 1960s, *Petticoat Junction* and its sister series *Green Acres*. Hooterville is a small farming community inhabited by a cast of oddball characters who are geographically and mentally removed from the rest of the world. Al-

though its exact location is never revealed, the remote town is surrounded by cornfields and small hills, suggesting it's located somewhere in the Midwest, yet there is no snow and it has 80-degree weather at Christmastime. What we do know about Hooterville is that it's in "The Kangaroo State," the land is prime for growing rutabagas, the elevation is 1,427 feet, and no one living outside of Hooterville Valley has ever heard of the town. In fact, Hooterville has been without a state government representative for forty years!

Hooterville was founded in 1868 by Horace Hooter, who arrived from Sacramento, California, with eight hundred dollars in his pocket to buy a farm. He meets his future wife Doris, a card shark with a Hungarian accent, in a saloon. She uses the eight hundred dollars to pay back the money she swindled, then wins it back playing cards. Horace buys a farm (which looks exactly like Oliver

---

Hooterville at a Glance

Where to Stay:
The Shady Rest Hotel $

Where to Eat:
The Pixley Diner $

Where to Shop:
Sam Drucker's General Store

Local Newspaper:
Hooterville World Guardian

Visitors to the Shady Rest Hotel always get a friendly welcome from (top row, left to right) Floyd Smoot (Rufe Davis), Kate Bradley (Bea Benaderet), Uncle Joe Carson (Edgar Buchanan), Charlie Pratt (Smiley Burnette), Bottom row: Bobbie Jo (Pat Woodell), Billie Jo (Jeannine Riley), and Betty Jo (Linda Kaye Henning).

and Lisa Douglas' place) and discusses with his neighbors the prospect of starting their own community. They try to think of a name (Hooter Heights?) and when they can't, Doris assures them that "Mr. Hooter vill"—which is how the town got its name!

The town is connected to the neighboring (and rival town) of Pixley by the main line of the C. F. & W. Railroad, along which runs the Hooterville Cannonball. At the helm of the steam engine are a pair of engineers, Charlie Pratt and Floyd Smoot. The train used in the interiors for *Petticoat Junction* was a replica of a 1901 model. It was built on a soundstage at General Studios in Hollywood, where both series were filmed. The real train, which was in Sonora, California, was used for the exterior shots.

Petticoat Junction is set at the Shady Rest, an old-fashioned, family-run hotel located along the railroad tracks. The establishment is owned and operated by an optimistic widow named Kate Bradley, who receives very little help from her lazy Uncle Joe. Kate has three attractive daughters—Billie Jo, Bobbie Jo, and Betty Jo—who do most of the work around the hotel. The Shady Rest was built in the middle of nowhere because Kate's grandfather, Mellard P. Bradley, was planning to build his hotel in Pixley, but when the flat cars hauling the lumber tipped over, he decided to build the hotel where the lumber was. Room number 7, the Mellard P. Bradley Suite, was named in his honor. The Shady Rest is constantly in danger of getting shut down, either because of a lack of business or by public enemy number one: the evil Homer Bedloe of the C.F. & W. Railroad Company. Bedloe would like nothing better than to dismantle the Cannonball and put the Shady Rest out of business, but his schemes never seem to work.

Green Acres focuses on the other side of town, where a New York lawyer lives with his Hungarian wife in a small, run-down farmhouse. Oliver Wendell Douglas and his wife Lisa Douglas made their first mistake when they answered an ad in *The Farm Gazette* and purchased a farm sight unseen from Mr. Haney. The place turns out to be a dump (the bedroom is missing a wall), but Oliver convinces his wife to stick it out for six

Hooterville in Jamestown, California

Railtown
5th Avenue and Reservoir Road
209-984-3954
Located southeast of Sacramento, this state park is devoted to steam and diesel trains that are on display for the public. The Number 3 train, built in 1891, was used for the exterior shots of the Cannonball.

months. Although he is not very successful as a farmer (perhaps its because he does it wearing a shirt, vest, and tie), Oliver is passionate about farming and he has a tendency to make long speeches about the American farmer's contribution to our nation's history.

Lisa, a Hungarian native who never quite mastered the English language, has trouble adjusting to country living. Dressed in her designer gowns, she is a disaster in the kitchen. Lisa spends most of her time preparing her own concoctions, usually variations on the only thing she knows how to make—"hotscakes"—such as Italian pancake pizza and hots-ka-bobs.

The people of Hooterville are not backward folks. They simply have their own way of doing things. The plots of *Green Acres* focus on how an impatient Oliver deals with the eccentricities of Hoovervillians, who are a constant source of frustration. The Doug-

Farm living is the life for Oliver Douglas (Eddie Albert), but not for his wife Lisa (Eva Gabor).

las' farmhand, Eb, who calls Oliver "Dad," is sweet, naive, and incompetent. Mr. Haney, a peddler, will sell anything to anybody for a price. He somehow manages to have exactly what you need for any occasion (catering service, travel agency) or to solve any problem (rainmaker, egg laying machine, soybean planter). Then there's Hank Kimball, a county agent, with a short-term memory problem who has difficulty answering the simplest of questions. Perhaps the duo who most continually raised Oliver's stress level were the Monroe Brothers: Alf and his sister Ralph. Oliver hired the incompetent carpenters to repair the farmhouse and the barn, but they never seem to quite get around to it, probably because they have no idea what they are doing.

The center of Hooterville is Sam Drucker's General Store, where the Bradleys and the Douglases shop. Drucker, who appeared regularly in both series, serves as the town's mayor, justice of the peace, deputy sheriff, publisher of the local newspaper, and school board president. He is more sensible than the other townspeople, though he certainly has an eccentric side. Drucker serves as the postmaster of Hooterville and one day a year, better known as "Old Mail Day," he delivers to Hootervillians all the letters and packages that were accidentally misplaced or fell behind a shelf.

Hooterville's most famous resident is a pig named Arnold, who is owned by farmer Fred Ziffel and his wife Doris. Oliver was perplexed by the way the Ziffels treat Arnold like a son. He was even more surprised to see the pig watching television (he could turn the set on himself), go to school, get drafted into the army, and become the heir of a $20 million estate.

Although Hooterville is remote, its citizens keep themselves occupied when they are not sitting around chewing the fat at Drucker's General Store. There are more parades than fires in Hooterville, so the men who belong to the Volunteer Fire Department must also play a marching band instrument so they can play in the Volunteer Fire Department Band (the band was formed *before* the department). In an attempt to bring some culture to the valley, Lisa and the other members of the Every-Other-Wednesday-Afternoon-Discussion-Club try to teach the band how to play Brahm's *Lullaby*. Although most of the citizens of Hooterville seem to be over forty, the younger residents (including Eb) are members of the Hooterville Young People's Agricultural Society.

RECOMMENDED VIEWING

To get a feel for life in Hooterville, the following episodes are recommended:

PETTICOAT JUNCTION

"The Country Fair"
Writers: Lila Garret and Bernie Kahn
Director: Hollingsworth Morse

Everyone is geared up for the annual Hooterville country fair: Bobbie Jo is singing in the talent contest ("Beautiful Dreamer"); Betty Jo is in charge of the Hooterville High entry in the pet contest (a pig named Everett); Kate defends her seven-year championship in the cake baking competition (with her Pineapple Upside-Down Highriser); and Uncle Joe is wreaking havoc for all of them. Original airdate: 2/8/66

"The Golden Spike Ceremony"
Writers: Charles Stewart and Dick Conway
Director: Elliot Lewis

Uncle Joe and a citizens committee plan to commemorate the seventy-fifth anniversary of the driving of the Golden Spike, which marked the completion of the Cannonball Railroad and the linking of Hooterville and Pixley. When they accidentally strike oil during the ceremony, Uncle Joe is convinced he's a millionaire. Original airdate: 12/20/69

GREEN ACRES

"The Case of the Hooterville Refund Fraud"
Writers: Jay Sommers and Dick Chevillat
Director: Richard L. Bare

When the citizens of Hooterville see the size of Oliver's tax refund due to his reported loss, they write in for refunds. Due to a computer glitch, the IRS shells out over $500,000, which they immediately spend. Now they have to find a raise some money—fast! Original airdate: 2/28/70

"The Rutabaga Story"
Writers: Jay Sommers and Dick Chevillat
Director: Richard L. Bare

When Oliver encourages all the farmers in the valley to plant rutabagas, they decide to turn Hooterville into the Rutabaga Capital, which they advertise by having Lisa ride across the country in a hot air balloon. Original airdate: 3/20/68

Petticoat Junction

Premiere Airdate: September 24, 1963
CBS   222 Episodes

Cast

Kate Bradley........ Bea Benaderet (1963–68)	Betty Jo Bradley Elliot .... Linda Kaye Henning
Uncle Joe Carson.......... Edgar Buchanan	Charlie Pratt .... Smiley Burnette (1963–67)
Billie Jo Bradley..... Jeannine Riley (1963–65)	Floyd Smoot .... Rufe Davis (1963–68)
.... Gunilla Hutton (1965–66)	Homer Bedloe .... Charles Lane (1963–68)
.... Meredith MacRae (1966–70)	Sam Drucker .... Frank Cady
Bobbie Jo Bradley ..... Pat Woodell (1963–65)	Steve Elliot .... Mike Minor (1966–70)
.... Lori Saunders (1965–70)	Dr. Janet Craig....... June Lockhart (1968–70)

Green Acres

Premiere Airdate: September 15, 1965
CBS   170 Episodes

Cast

Oliver Wendell Douglas.......... Eddie Albert	Fred Ziffel .... Hank Patterson
Lisa Douglas .... Eva Gabor	Doris Ziffel........ Barbara Pepper (1965–69)
Mr. Haney .... Pat Buttram	.... Fran Ryan (1969–70)
Eb Dawson .... Tom Lester	Newt Kiley .... Kay E. Kuter (1965–70)
Hank Kimball .... Alvy Moore	Alf Monroe............ Sid Melton (1965–79)
Sam Drucker .... Frank Cady	Ralph Monroe .... Mary Grace Canfield

A little town in Vermont

Newhart (1982–90)

Created by Barry Kemp

A Manhattan couple, Dick and Joanna Loudon, have decided to make a major change in their lives. They are moving to Vermont to become the new proprietors of the Stratford, a slightly run-down colonial inn. Dick is a self-admitted history buff and the successful author of how-to books (including *Building Your Own Patio Cover, The Joy of Tubing,* and *Know Your Harley*), while Joanna does charity work (for several diseases). Neither of them has any experience as innkeepers, let alone restoring an inn that is badly in need of repair. Fortunately (or unfortunately), they receive some help from their not-so-handy handyman George Utley, whose family has been taking care of the Stratford for years. Dick and Joanna slowly realize they will need some time to adjust to small town life.

It may be difficult to pinpoint the exact location of Bob Newhart's second successful sitcom on a state map. During its eight-year run, the name of the town in which the Stratford is located was never mentioned. According to series creator Barry Kemp, one can assume the name of the town is Stratford, located approximately one mile

---

A little town in Vermont at a Glance

Where to Stay:
The Stratford Inn $$

Where to Eat:
The Minuteman Café $

Local Media:
WPIV-TV

The Official Town Fish:
The flounder

The Official Bird:
The flying squirrel

Visitors to the Stratford Inn are greeted by its proprietor, Dick Loudon (Bob Newhart).

George Utley (Tom Poston, left) is one in a long line of Utleys who have served as the Stratford Inn's handymen.

across the Vermont/New Hampshire border from Dartmouth College, which is in Hanover, New Hampshire. The closest Vermont town to Hanover is Norwich, which is sometimes listed as the setting of the show, though the producers never actually revealed the town's location.

The history of the Stratford Inn itself is quite clear. According to Dick, the inn was built in 1774 by Nathan Potter, who named it the Stratford after his ancestor's home in England. Potter died two months later, so the inn was sold. The Daughters of the War for Independence believe the inn has historic value because many of their ancestors stayed there in the winter of 1775. Dick reluctantly reveals, when addressing the ladies of the DWI, that at the time the Stratford was actually a brothel.

Another unpleasant piece of history is discovered. Everyone in the town, except Dick and Joanna, know that the three hundred-year old corpse of Sarah Newton (1660–92) is in the basement of the Stratford Inn. She was refused burial alongside her husband in the church cemetery because she was hanged for being a witch. To move Mrs. Newton's body, the Loudons enlist the help of three backwoods bumpkin brothers who will do anything for a buck—Larry, his brother Darryl, and his other brother Darryl. At the last minute, the Loudons decide it's only fair to let Sarah Newton's remains stay in the basement.

Next door to the inn is the Minuteman Café and Souvenir Shop, owned for the first two seasons by a self-admitted compulsive liar named Kirk Devane. Kirk has his eye on the Stratford's maid, Leslie Vanderkellen, a rich Dartmouth student (her father owns an island on the Caribbean and she has her own foundation) who took the job because she wanted to find out what it's like to be "average." Leslie is overqualified for the maid job. She's earning her masters degree in Renaissance Theory and is practicing to be on the Olympic ski team. When Leslie decides to study in England, her cousin Stephanie, a spoiled princess who is even less qualified to do housework, takes over the job after she leaves her husband after two days of marriage.

A Little Town in Vermont in East Middlebury, Vermont

The Waybury Inn
Route 125 East
(800) 348-1810
The Waybury Inn was used for the exterior shots of the Stratford Inn. Founded in 1810, it was originally a tavern and still houses a pub today. Poet Robert Frost often stayed there in the 1950s and early 1960s.

When Kirk blows out of town to marry Cindy, a professional clown, the Minuteman Café is bought by Larry and the Darryls. They enlist Joanna's help when they find that their lack of social graces is keeping the customers away. Joanna redecorates the café and gives them some pointers on how to serve customers, but in the end, she learns you can't make a silk purse out of a sow's ear. Dick also thinks he has a handle on Vermont living, but, like Joanna, he can get overzealous and find himself off the mark when it comes to fitting in with the locals. When he is asked to run for town council, he dresses too casually for the first meeting and discovers there are no elections and the town council meets only once a year. Dick is also skeptical about the local legend of the Great White Buck, which, if spotted, brings good luck to the town. When he finally spots it for himself, he accidentally kills it with his car, which brings bad luck to the town. To reverse the curse, Dick is forced to don antlers in front of the town and perform a wood nymph dance.

Dick also became a local celebrity when he was hired to host *Vermont Today*, a talk show on the local station, WPIV-TV. At one point, his show was canceled and replaced with a new, hipper one titled *On the Town*. Bob was paired with a perky co-host, but luckily for him, the new format didn't last too long and he went back to hosting *Vermont Today*.

Did You Know?

The series was videotaped during the first season, but switched over to film the following year because it gave the series a classier look and all the other sitcoms in the Monday night line-up were filmed.

Larry, his brother Darryl, and his other brother Darryl were only set to appear in one episode, but they became so popular that they were upgraded to series regulars in the third season.

Tom Poston, who played George, was an old friend of Bob Newhart's. He had appeared on *The Bob Newhart Show* as Bob's friend, Cliff "The Peeper" Murdock.

Mary Frann died unexpectedly of a heart attack on September 23, 1998.

One source of frustration for Bob at the station and at home was his fast-talking producer, Michael Harris, who became involved with and eventually married Stephanie.

The final episode of the series is one of the most memorable half hours on television. On the 216th birthday of the Stratford, a Japanese investor offers to buy the inn and the rest of the town for a million dollars per house so he can build a very large golf course. Dick refuses to sell, leaving the Loudons the only ones left in the town. In a flash-forward to five years in the future, we find that the Stratford has been transformed into a Japanese-style hotel and Joanna is wearing a kimono. When Dick is hit with a golf ball, he wakes up in the middle of the night, revealing Newhart's wife from his previous series, Emily Hartley (played by Suzanne Pleshette), in bed next to him. Dick describes a dream he had in which he was an innkeeper—implying the entire series was psychiatrist Bob Hartley's dream.

RECOMMENDED VIEWING

To get a feel for life in this little town in Vermont, the following episodes of *Newhart* are recommended:

"The Pilot"
Writer: Barry Kemp
Director: John Rich
Dick and Joanna set up housekeeping at the Stratford and welcome their first guests.

The highlight: Dick's speech on the history of the Stratford to the Daughters of the War for Independence. Original airdate: 10/25/82

"Hail to the Councilman"
Writer: Sheldon Bull
Director: Will Mackenzie

Although he has only been in town for a few weeks, Dick is asked to run for town council. When Dick and Joanna attend a meeting, they get to experience local politics first-hand. Original airdate: 11/8/82

"Candidate Larry"
Writer: Douglas Wyman
Director: Dick Martin

Larry decides to run for mayor and feels betrayed when Dick decides to support another candidate. Original airdate: 11/4/85

"The Last Newhart"
Writers: Mark Egan, Mark Solomon, and Bob Bendetson
Director: Dick Martin

While the rest of the town sells their property to the Japanese, Dick and Joanna refuse to give up the Stratford. The last scene is one of TV's classic comedy moments. Original airdate: 5/21/90

Newhart

Premiere Airdate: October 25, 1982
CBS   184 Episodes

Cast

Dick Loudon . . . . Bob Newhart	Stephanie Vanderkellen . . Julia Duffy (1983–90)
Joanna Loudon . . . . Mary Frann	Larry. . . . . William Sanderson
George Utley . . . . Tom Poston	Darryl #1 . . . . Tony Papenfuss
Kirk Devane . . . . . Steven Kampmann (1982–84)	Darryl #2 . . . . John Voldstad
Leslie Vanderkellen	Michael Harris. . . . . . . Peter Scolari (1984–90)
. . . . . . Jennifer Holmes (1982–83)	

Llanview, Pennsylvania

One Life to Live (1968–Present)

Created by Agnes Nixon

There must be something special about the city of Llanview, Pennsylvania. Over the years, this mid-size metropolis has been the home of not one but two rich, influential men, newspaper mogul Victor Lord and Texan oil baron Asa Buchanan. Llanview is certainly a nice place to live and raise a family, or, in Victor and Asa's cases, *control* a family.

When *One Life to Live* premiered in 1968, the soap was praised for the diversity of its characters in terms of their ethnicity, race, and class. Storylines revolved around the conflict created when characters fell in love with people out of their "element." Victor Lord was far from pleased when his daughter, Victoria, fell in love with a middle-class Irishman, Joe Riley, while her sister Meredith set her sights on Dr. Larry Wolek, who was from a working-class Polish-American family. Another story line involved a light-skinned black woman who passed herself off as Italian.

Llanview remains one of daytime television's most diverse communities. The Buchanans and the Lords (minus Victor) still reside in Llanview. Living and working alongside these prominent families are the

---

Llanview at a Glance

Where to Stay:
The Palace Hotel $$$

Where to Eat:
The Palace Hotel Restaurant $$$
Carlotta's Diner $

Favorite Hangout:
Rodi's Tavern

Local Newspapers:
The Banner
The Sun

Local TV Station:
WVLE-TV

When counterfeiter Ted Clayton put a contract out on their lives, Marco Dane (Gerald Anthony) and Karen Wolek (Judith Light) escaped along Llanview's deserted railroad tracks.

Llanview's resident heroine Vicki Lord (Erika Slezak, left) with Maggie Ashley (Jacqueline Courtney).

Vega family, who live in the Angel Square district of Llanview, on the east side of town. In the 1990s, *One Life to Live* became one of daytime's most socially-aware soaps, dealing with controversial topics such as homophobia, AIDS, and teenage gangs.

Llanfair, an eighteenth-century mansion, is the home of heroine Victoria Lord, publisher and owner of Llanview's most respected newspaper, *The Banner*. Her son Kevin, who resides in Llanfair's carriage house, is its editor-in-chief. Victoria has been treated for dissociative identity disorder caused by the sexual abuse she experienced as a child by her father. While she was one manifesting one of her personalities (nineteen-year-old Tori), she burned down Llanfair, but managed to switch back to being Vicki in time to save her daughter Jessica (four years earlier, little Jessica had accidentally set fire to Llanfair). Vicki always blamed the death of her beloved father on her former stepmother and arch enemy, Dorian Lord, but when Vicki finally discovered that she had been abused by him, she found that one of her several personalities had killed him. Victoria has been plagued by other health problems, including an aneurysm. While in a coma, she enjoyed a brief stay in heaven and was reunited with her late husband, Joe Riley. When Victoria was mayor of Llanview, she went up against Llanview's crime lord, Carlo Hesser (a.k.a. Poseidon), who ran the city's drug trade. Vicki was shot by an assassin and suffered a stroke after the shooting, which left her paralyzed. Once again she managed to recover.

The Lords may be one of the most respected families in town, but the Buchanans are the richest in Llanview (and the whole state of Pennsylvania). Asa Buchanan, who made his fortune in oil, is CEO of Buchanan Enterprises. He is a shrewd businessman who will stop at nothing to get his own way. In the past, he held the first of his many wives prisoner in Moor Cliffe mansion, faked his own death, and went to prison for withholding evidence. Asa most recently married wife number nine, Renee Divine, who was also wife number six and a former madame. Renee, who lives with her husband in the

Buchanan mansion, has gone from running a bordello to being the owner of Llanview's ritziest hotel and restaurant, the Palace.

The Palace Hotel is also the home of Asa's son, Bo. One of his many past occupations was police commissioner of Llanview. Before he started enforcing the law, Bo was executive producer of a locally produced soap opera, *Fraternity Row*, for WVLE-TV. While the series was being shot on location at Llanview University (actually it was the campus of Duke University), a stalker began terrorizing the cast and crew. Bo apprehended the lunatic, who turned out to be a production assistant (no doubt underpaid) on the show.

Llanview has been paralyzed by several rapists and stalkers. One high-profile trial involved the gang rape of Marty Saybrooke by three Llanview University fraternity brothers, Zach Rosen, Powell Lord III, and Llanview's resident bad boy (and star quarterback) Todd Manning. When a mistrial was declared, Todd attacked Marty again, but was caught and ended up in jail, from which he would later escape. Meanwhile, a masked rapist began to terrorize women working at Llanview Hospital. Ironically it was Todd, everyone's chief suspect, who captured the culprit—his former Kappa Alpha Delta fraternity bro, Powell. Over the next few years, Todd would continue to terrorize Llanview. In addition to rape, his rap sheet includes kidnapping, assault, and bombing. When he discovered he was Victor Lord's son and the true heir to the Lord fortune, he went up against his step-sister Vicki and

Buchanan family patriarch Asa (Philip Carey) with sons Bo (Robert S. Woods) and Clint (Clint Ritchie).

bought the *Banner's* rival paper, the *Intruder*, from Dorian and renamed it the *Sun*.

Llanview residents living on the other side of the tracks are certainly not immune to violence. The Angel Street Community Center, located in East Llanview, which had recently been renovated by Marty Saybrooke and her new beau, Dylan Moody, became a battleground between two local rival gangs, the Arrows and the Prides. When the Arrows tried to control Angel Square, the Prides became the defenders of the community. The murder of Dylan's sister Luna by a gang member sparked a gang war in Angel Square. The violence came to an end when Police Commissioner Bo Buchanan discovered it had been one of his own men, Detective Manzo, who had been selling guns to gang members.

Peace was restored for a short time on Angel Square, where residents often visit the CK Diner, run by Carlotta Vega, the matriarch of the Vega family. The area once again fell under siege, this time by Asa Buchanan, who planned to build a strip mall in the area. The project was abandoned when Asa was unable to purchase one piece of property he needed—a warehouse owned by Dorian. Out of spite, Dorian sold it to Maggie Carpenter, who planned to build a clown school. When the warehouse was destroyed by fire, Maggie's dream of training the future Bozos of America when up in flames.

Some of Llanview's residents find time to

Viki (Erika Slezak) gets help from Dr. Larry Wolek (Michael Stor, left) and Clint (Clint Ritchie).

go to church (most have a reason to) and seek the spiritual advice of Reverend Andrew Carpenter of St. James Church. Reverend Carpenter became the focus of a scandal in Llanview when he counseled a gay teenager, Billy Douglas. A wave of homophobia hit the town when Marty Saybrooke, who had a crush on Andrew, spread a rumor that the reverend seduced Billy. Andrew became the target of violent and hate, but he taught the town a lesson in tolerance when he publicly disclosed that his own brother, William, was gay and had died of AIDS. When Andrew arranged for the AIDS quilt to come to Llanview, he added a panel for his brother.

Llanview is nestled on the Llatano River below nearby Llatano Mountain (all the major locations on *One Life to Live* seem to begin with a double L). The mountain was the site of the wedding between Irish poet Patrick Thornhart and Marty Saybrooke. Unfortunately the wedding was disrupted by IRA terrorists. Llatano Mountain was also the site of the lost city of Eterna, which served as a storage facility for Victor Lord's money. Several characters were trapped in the city, but they managed to escape before Eterna collapsed.

One Life to Live

Premiere Airdate: July 15, 1968
ABC

Cast

Asa Buchanan	Philip Carey	Victoria Lord Carpenter	Erika Slezak
Bo Buchanan	Robert S. Woods	Jessica Buchanan	Erin Torpey
Cassie Carpenter	Laura Bonariggo	Lindsay Rappaport	Catherine Hickland
Dorian Cramer Lord	Robin Strasser	Kevin Buchanan	Timothy Gibbs
Renee Divine	Patricia Elliot	Carlotta Vega	Patricia Mauceri

Mayberry, North Carolina

The Andy Griffith Show (1960–68)

Created by Sheldon Leonard (with Andy Griffith & Aaron Ruben)

Mayberry, R.F.D. (1968–71)

Created by Bob Ross

Mayberry at a Glance

Nickname:
Garden City of the State

Where to Stay:
The Mayberry Hotel $$

Where to Dine:
Morelli's (try the pounded steak!) $$
The Bluebird Diner $
The Snappy Lunch $

Where to Shop:
Weaver's Department Store

Local Newspaper:
The Mayberry Gazette

In one of the most memorable episodes of *The Andy Griffith Show*, Malcolm Tucker (played by guest star Robert Emhardt), a businessman on his way to Charlotte, has car trouble on the outskirts of Mayberry. Malcolm runs into a bit more bad luck because it's Sunday and the good folks of Mayberry are taking it nice and slow. Frustrated because he can't get a mechanic to work on his car, Malcolm cries out: "You people are living in another world! This is the twentieth century! Don't you realize that?" After spending the afternoon with the Taylors—Sheriff Andy, his son Opie, his Aunt Bee, and his cousin Deputy Barney Fife—Malcolm begins to appreciate the slow pace of Mayberry. When his car gets fixed later that afternoon, he decides to stay the night with the Taylors.

Perhaps it's that down-home feeling that

Myers Lake is the perfect place for Andy (Andy Griffith) and Opie (Ron Howard) to spend a Saturday afternoon.

The streets of Mayberry are kept safe by the town's top-notch law enforcers: Sheriff Andy Taylor (Andy Griffith) and Deputy Barney Fife (Don Knotts).

kept audiences tuning in Monday nights for eleven years to watch what was happening (and not happening) in the peaceful, sleepy town of Mayberry. *The Andy Griffith Show* (and its successor, *Mayberry, R.F.D.*) sustained its popularity during one of the most turbulent decades in American history. Political assassinations, the civil rights movement, and student protests over the Vietnam War seemed to have no effect on life in Mayberry County. While Andy Taylor was sheriff, Mayberry's

murder rate remained at zero percent and the occasional nonviolent crime was limited to moonshining, public drunkenness, shoplifting, jaywalking, gambling, pick pocketing, counterfeiting, and burglary. In fact, Andy never even carried a gun because he wanted Mayberrians to respect rather than fear him. This sense of peacefulness and security is the reason *The Andy Griffith Show* was so popular with viewers (and remains so even today).

Mayberry is called "The Friendly Town" for a reason. It is inhabited by an array of colorful, folksy characters who can be found, on a typical day, on Main Street, the hub of Mayberry. Andy Taylor is usually in the sheriff's station if he's not hanging out with county clerk Howard Sprague in Floyd Lawson's barbershop or getting his patrol car filled up by Gomer Pyle at Wally's Service Station. There are dozens of other familiar faces, including Aunt Bee's best friend, Clara Johnson; Barney's steady girl, Thelma Lou; and the town gossip, Emma Brand Watson. Visitors like Malcolm Tucker are, of course, always welcome and many episodes revolve around an outsider who comes to town to visit relatives or, in some instances, stirs up trouble, like an occasional swindler or escaped convict.

Mayberry may be a quiet place, but there is plenty to do. Most Mayberrians are active in a variety of civic organizations, such as the Good Government League, the Women's Historical Society, and Andy's lodge, The Regal Order of the Golden Door to Good Fellowship. There are also social events, such as picnics and dances sponsored by the All Souls Church (where Andy and Barney sing

Did You Know?

The Andy Griffith Show was a spinoff of *The Danny Thomas Show*. Thomas' character, entertainer Danny Williams, is arrested by Sheriff Taylor for driving through a stop sign. Ronny Howard appears as Opie and Frances Bavier plays the town widow, Henrietta Perkins. During the commercial break, Thomas and Griffith appear together in a commercial for the show's sponsor, Maxwell House Instant Coffee.

Some of the familiar faces who have made an appearance in Mayberry include Rob Reiner (as Joe, the typesetter at Hammond's Print Shop), Teri Garr (as a customer at Goober's filling station), Don Rickles (as Newton Monroe, a traveling salesman), Barbara Eden (as Ellen Brown, a sexy manicurist), and Jack Nicholson (as Mr. Garland, the father of the baby Opie finds, and as Marvin Jenkins, a burglary suspect whom juror Aunt Bee believes is innocent).

R.F.D. stands for "Rural Free Delivery."

Two-time Academy Award winner Jodie Foster made three appearances on *Mayberry, R.F.D.* alongside her brother Buddy, who played Mike Jones.

After leaving Mayberry, Andy (Andy Griffith) returned for a visit with *Mayberry R.F.D.*'s Sam Jones (Ken Berry).

in the choir), the Chamber of Commerce, and the Women's Club. Recreational events include fishing at Myer's Lake, local Little League games at Mayberry Field, and the occasional game of checkers or dominoes.

Like many southern towns, Mayberry is rich in history. Several episodes have focused on the historical events that took place in and around the town. According to the events reenacted in the 1962 Centennial Pageant (which should be a Bicentennial Pageant since the Battle of Mayberry was fought in 1762), Mayberry was settled by a group of pioneers, including the town's namesake, John Mayberry. As the story goes, one of the pioneers, James Merriweather, smoked a peace pipe with an Indian chief named Noogatuck. The two pledged that the Indians and settlers would live together in harmony. During the Revolutionary War, a soldier named Nathan Tibbs (a forebear of Otis Campbell, the town drunk) ran eight miles through the snow and burned down the Mayberry Bridge. The enemy was prevented from crossing and Washington's men captured an entire regiment.

The most significant moment in town's history is the Battle of Mayberry. Andy, Gomer, Clara Edwards, and Sarah, the (unseen) telephone operator, all claim to have ancestors who were colonels involved in the legendary battle with Cherokee Indians, who defended their land under the leadership of Chief Strongbow. The battle, it turns out, wasn't really much of a battle at all. While writing an essay for a contest sponsored by *The Mayberry Gazette*, Opie discovered in a Raleigh

The residents of Mayberry, R.F.D.: Sam Jones (Ken Berry), his son Mike (Buddy Foster), and girlfriend Millie Hutchins (Arlene Golonka).

Did You Know?

Neil Brower, a United Methodist minister and author of the book, *Mayberry 101* teaches a ten-week course on the show. He is also a member of *The Andy Griffith Show* Rerun Watchers Club, which has over one thousand chapters and twenty thousand members around the country.

142 miles from Raleigh, the state capitol. Several popular characters and establishments in the fictitious town of Mayberry, such as the Snappy Lunch and the Grand Theatre, were named after actual places Griffith frequented as a child. Mayberry is located in the same area of the state in fictitious Mayberry County, though Raleigh, depending on the episode, is either fifty-five, sixty, or one hundred miles away. The streets of Mayberry were actually located at Forty Acres, a studio backlot in Culver City, California. The interiors were shot at Desilu Studios in Hollywood and the country exteriors (including the title sequence) were filmed in Franklin Canyon in the Hollywood Hills.

When Andy Griffith decided to hang up his sheriff's hat, Mayberry continued at the same slow pace. Toward the end of the eighth season, two new characters, a widower named Sam Jones, who lives on a farm in Mayberry, and his eight-year-old son Mike, were introduced. The head of the Mayberry town council, Sam, like Andy, approaches problems with patience and common sense and is a devoted father to his son. The Jones family became the focus of the spinoff, *Mayberry, R.F.D.*, which lasted three seasons.

The original cast of *The Andy Griffith Show* was reunited for a 1986 made-for-TV movie, *Return to Mayberry*. Andy returns to Mayberry after twenty years to get his old job back, only to find Barney in a heated race for sheriff. In the end, Andy and Barney assume their original jobs as sheriff and deputy. Frances Bavier, who retired from show business, chose not to appear in the telefilm.

newspaper that the great battle involved an exchange of insults between the settlers and the Indians, all of whom got drunk on corn liquor. The only casualties were a cow, three deer, and a mule. The *Gazette* printed Opie's essay and the town was congratulated by the governor of North Carolina for its honesty.

Mayberry was modeled on Andy Griffith's hometown—Mount Airy, North Carolina. The town is located in the northwest portion of the state near the Virginia border,

RECOMMENDED VIEWING

To get a feel for life in Mayberry, the following episodes are recommended:

THE ANDY GRIFFITH SHOW

"Mayberry Goes Hollywood"
Writers: Benedict Freeman and
    John Fenton Murray
Director: Bob Sweeny

A Hollywood movie producer wants to use Mayberry, a quiet and peaceful all-American town, as the setting of his next film. The townspeople, except for Andy, get caught up in the excitement and begin to Hollywood-ize their little town. Original airdate: 1/2/61

"Man in a Hurry"
Writers: Everett Greenbaum and
    Jim Fritzell
Director: Bob Sweeny

On his way to Charlotte, businessman Malcolm Tucker's (Robert Emhardt) car breaks down in Mayberry. After spending an afternoon with the Taylors and the good folks of Mayberry, he decides to take life a little slower. Original airdate: 1/14/63

"Sermon For a Day"
Writer: John Whedon
Director: Dick Crenna

A Reverend (David Lewis) visiting from New York poses a question to a Mayberry congregation: "What's your hurry?" Andy and company follow the reverend's advice and try to take time and enjoy life by staging an old-fashioned band concert in the park. The project requires more work than they imagine. Original airdate: 10/21/63

MAYBERRY, R.F.D.

"The Panel Show"
Writer: Joseph Bonaduce
Director: Hal Cooper

Emmett and Howard are selected as representatives of Mayberry to go to New York and participate on a talk show, *Talk It Up,* to defend small town life. When he arrives in town, Howard transforms himself into a mod city slicker. On the program, he begins to praise the advantage of big city living. The folks of Mayberry turn on him, but all is forgiven when Howard asks for forgiveness in a poem in which he describes Mayberry as paradise. Original airdate: 10/28/68

"New Couple in Town"
Writer: Dan Beaumont
Director: Hal Cooper

The members of Aunt Bee's literary club reject Goober Pyle's application to join because he only reads comic books. When a writer named Frank Wylie moves to Mayberry, the club is thrilled to find out the town has its own resident author—only to discover that Mr. Wylie writes comic books. Original airdate: 1/6/69

"Sister Cities"
Writer: Albert E. Lewin
Director: Hal Cooper

Mayberry is chosen by the state department to be sister city of Puerto Bello, Mexico. The mayor and town council of Puerto Bello come for a visit and to make a good impression, they present Mayberry with an expensive gift. When Sam discovers that the Mexican town, like Mayberry, is relatively poor, they return the gift and present the mayor with a small token of their friendship—a needlepoint sampler created by Aunt Bee declaring "God Bless Puerto Bello." Original airdate: 5/12/69

The Andy Griffith Show

Premiere Airdate: October 3, 1960
CBS   249 Episodes

Cast

Andy Taylor	Andy Griffith	Gomer Pyle	Jim Nabors (1963–64)
Aunt Bee	Frances Bavier	Goober Pyle	George Lindsay (1965–68)
Opie Taylor	Ronny Howard	Howard Sprague	Jack Dodson
Barney Fife	Don Knotts (1960–65)	Thelma Lou	Betty Lynn (1960–65)
Floyd Lawson	Howard McNear	Warren Ferguson	Jack Burns (1965–66)
Otis Campbell	Hal Smith (1960–67)		

Mayberry, R.F.D.

Premiere Airdate: September 26, 1968
CBS   78 Episodes

Cast

Sam Jones	Ken Berry	Millie Hutchins	Arlene Golonka
Mike Jones	Buddy Foster	Alice Cooper	Alice Ghostley (1970–71)
Aunt Bee	Frances Bavier (1968–70)	Howard Sprague	Jack Dodson
Goober Pyle	George Lindsay	Emmett Clark	Paul Hartman

Wally (Tony Dow) consoles the Beaver (Jerry Mathers) when he has a bad hair day.

Mayfield

Leave It to Beaver (1957–63)

Created by Joe Connelly and Bob Mosher

Still the Beaver (1985–86)
The New Leave It to Beaver (1986–89)

Mayfield at a Glance

Where to Stay:
The Mayfield Hotel $$$

Where to Dine:
The White Fox $$$
Mayfield Country Club $$$

Where to Shop:
Parker's Pet Store
Uncle Artie's Magic Shop
The Book Nook

Where to Play Ball:
Metzger's Field

Best Movie House:
The Mayfield Theater

Local Newspaper:
The Courier Sun
Mayfield Press

Like many comedies of the 1950s (*Ozzie and Harriet, Father Knows Best*), *Leave It to Beaver* was set in white, middle-class, suburban America. With its white picket-fenced houses and manicured lawns, Mayfield was television's idea of utopia for the emerging generation of baby boomers. Did anyone (besides Beaver Cleaver) actually grow up in a town like Mayfield? Did anyone toss around a football in the backyard with kids named Lumpy, Whitey, and Tooey, while Mom made sandwiches in the kitchen and Dad read his paper in the den? Any resemblance between *Leave It to Beaver* and real life was entirely coincidental. Yet, because there was something familiar and reassuring about the Cleavers—an all-American, squeaky clean family, in which the kids were always goofing off and the parents, even Dad, occasionally made mistakes—they have earned their place in television history.

When *Leave It to Beaver* premiered in

Beaver (Jerry Mathers) is surprised by a kiss from one of his admirers.

1957, the Cleavers—Ward, June, and their sons Wally and Theodore (a.k.a. Beaver)—lived in the town of Mayfield at 485 Maple Drive. They later moved to 211 Pine Street, an equally generic-sounding address. The exact location of Mayfield is a hotly debated topic among the show's loyal fans. Most believe Mayfield is located in Ohio because Shaker Heights, a suburb of Cleveland, and Cincinnati are frequently mentioned (though the latter is a long-distance phone call from Mayfield). The Ohio theory is questionable because the ocean is twenty minutes away and the boys visit Captain Jack's Alligator Farm in the first episodes, at which palm trees can be seen in the background. Wherever it is, Mayfield is not isolated from the rest of the world. Bellport (wherever that is) can be reached by train and Crystal Lake, where Beaver's friend Billy Payton lives, is a ninety-mile bus drive away.

While *Dobie Gillis* showed us life from a teenager's perspective, *Leave It to Beaver* presented the world from a child's point of view. The places we see or hear about in Mayfield are limited to the little corner of the world Beaver inhabits: the soda fountain at the local drugstore; the Mayfield movie theater; Friend's Lake, where Beaver and Larry unknowingly go for a ride in a stolen rowboat and Wally gets a job as a hotdog vendor; Miller's Pond, in which Beaver's homemade boat capsizes; the Mayfield Zoo, home

June (Barbara Billingsley) and Ward (Hugh Beaumont) Cleaver reminisce about their life in Mayfield.

Did You Know?

How Beaver got his name is explained in the final episode. Ward and June explain that when Wally was little, he couldn't pronounce Theodore—which came out sounding like Beaver.

The pilot for *Leave It to Beaver* was entitled *It's a Small World*. Jerry Mathers and Barbara Billingsley played Beaver and June, but Casey Adams was featured as Ward and Paul Sullivan was Wally. A very young Harry Shearer, who lends his voice to *The Simpsons*, played one of Wally's pals.

The show was originally shot at CBS Television City (formerly Republic Studios), but it later moved to Stage 17 of Universal Studios. If you take the tour at Universal Studios, you can see a replica of the Beaver house, which was used for the 1997 feature film version. The Cleavers' house is located directly across the street from the Munster's house, which was featured on *Beaver* as the McMahon house. The original Cleaver house was later seen on *Marcus Welby, M.D.* and *The Rockford Files*.

The cast of *Leave It to Beaver* has been the subject of several urban myths:

- Jerry Mathers was reported to have been killed in combat in Vietnam. Mathers was in the Air National Guard, but he never fought in Vietnam.

- Ken Osmond grew up to be Alice Cooper or porn star Johnny Holmes. Both rumors are false. Osmond did become a motorcycle traffic cop with the Los Angeles Police Department.

of Beaver's former pet monkey, Stanley; the McMahon place, Mayfield's official haunted house; and the Pink Room of the Mayfield Hotel, where poor Beaver and Larry are forced to take dance lessons from Miss Prescott on Saturday afternoons. Beaver is always coming up with get-rich-quick schemes (he even purchases a copy of *I Became a Millionaire in Twelve Months* as a gift for his dad). Most of his ideas, like becoming a model, peddling perfume, and selling water to Wally and his thirsty friends, backfire. This doesn't stop Beaver from spending money. He purchases a baby alligator through an ad in the back of a comic book and frequents several businesses around town, including the Book Nook (for comics), Nelson's Bakery, and Uncle Artie's Magic Shop. For free junk (literally), Beaver and his friends like to look through Fats Flannaghan's Junkyard on Euclid Avenue.

Beaver's older brother Wally has more common sense than his brother and is usually bailing him out of trouble. He is athletic, shy around girls, and concerned about making a good impression. He frequently takes girls out for "soda dates" at the local drugstore or a dance at Mayfield High School, the Mayfield Country Club, or the Mayfield Cotillion. Wally doesn't want to be treated like a kid, so he is often determined to make his own decisions. Yet he still has some growing up to do. When he asks Julie Foster out on a formal date, he takes her to the White Fox, not knowing it's one of the most expensive restaurants in Mayfield. His parents are always nearby to set things right, sometimes without Wally ever knowing it. As Ward tells June, "You are the master of the indirect approach." Like Beaver, Wally has his own group of friends, including the devious and smarmy Eddie Haskell, who is under the illusion he can cover his true nature by being polite and handing out compliments ("That's a very pretty dress you have on, Mrs. Cleaver").

June Cleaver is the original TV stay-at-home mom, who rarely leaves the house alone except to go to the market and attend Women's Club meetings. Ward Cleaver works in downtown Mayfield, but his occupation, like that of many television dads of this era, was never made clear. He is employed by a "firm," where he works with Lumpy's dad, Fred Rutherford (the firm's main office is in New York). He is active in the Mayfield community and attends the Mayfield Businessmen Luncheons. Ward frequently has to write "reports" at home, which leads many viewers to conclude he's an accountant. As he often tells June and his sons, Ward was raised on a farm (Mayfield must seem like a big city to him!). He is never short on fatherly advice, which he dispenses in a short-but-sweet fashion. The lessons are familiar—be yourself, tell the truth, be responsible, and so on. Ward is not perfect in the parent department, so when he makes a mistake, he often learns a lesson or two himself. For example, he and June assume the boys have blown off their paper route (for the *Courier Sun*) and decide to deliver the stack in the garage themselves, only to later discover they were last week's papers. When Ward catches Wally using his razor, he chews him out in front of Eddie Haskell, who gives Wally a new nickname—Baby Face. Ward apologizes to Wally for scolding him in front of his friend. He even becomes jealous when Wally and Beaver start spending time with Willie Dennison's father, so he puts up a basketball hoop in the backyard. The kids are reluctant to play at the Cleavers' house because Ward insists on joining in. Eventually he realizes a good father knows there are times when it's best to leave his kids alone.

The Cleaver family were reunited (minus Hugh Beaumont, who does appear in flashbacks) in 1983 for the made-for-TV-movie, *Still the Beaver*. In the film, Wally is an attorney who is happily married to his high school sweetheart, Mary Ellen Rogers. They are having trouble conceiving a child because Wally is impotent(!). After losing his job, house, car, and wife, Beaver moves back to Mayfield to live with his mother and fight for the custody of his kids. The film also featured characters from the original cast, including Eddie Haskell, Fred and Lumpy Rutherford, and Larry Mondello.

The success of the film led to a revival of the series, aptly titled *The New Leave It to Beaver*, which focused on the relationship between Beaver and Wally (now next-door neighbors) and their kids. Many members of the original cast were reunited. Beaver is now a single dad raising two sons, Kip and Oliver, and living back at home with June. He also goes into business with his childhood friend Lumpy and serves on the Mayfield City Council. Wally, his wife Ellen, and their two children, Kelly and Kevin, live nearby. Even Eddie Haskell is still living in Mayfield, raising his son Freddie, who followed in his father's footsteps as the most obnoxious kid in town.

RECOMMENDED VIEWING

To get a feel for life in Mayfield, the following episodes are recommended:

"Wally's New Suit"
Writer: Richard Baer
Director: Norman Tokar

Ward and June want Wally to buy a new suit for the upcoming dance. Wally insists on going alone to pick it out. He brings home a loud plaid suit, so June maneuvers him into exchanging it for more suitable threads. Original airdate: 12/4/58

"Borrowed Boat"
Writer: Joe Connelly and Bob Mosher
Director: Norman Tokar

Instead of going to Wally's basketball game, Beaver goes to Friend's Lake with Larry. The boys accept a free ride in a rowboat, which turns out to be stolen, and are arrested. Original airdate: 11/14/59

"In the Soup"
Writer: Dick Conway
Director: Norman Abbott

Beaver accepts a dare by Whitey and climbs up a billboard for Zesto soup ("The discriminating hostess serves Zesto Soup"), which has a large cup of soup with steam pouring out of it. To prove to Whitey there is not real soup in the cup, Beaver climbs in and can't get out. The entire neighborhood comes out to watch the fire department rescue Beaver. Original airdate: 5/6/61

Leave It to Beaver

Premiere Airdate: October 4, 1957
CBS (1957–59), ABC (1959–63)   234 Episodes

Cast

Beaver Cleaver . . . . Jerry Mathers
Ward Cleaver . . . . Hugh Beaumont
June Cleaver . . . . Barbara Billingsley
Wally Cleaver . . . . Tony Dow
Eddie Haskell . . . . Ken Osmond

Larry Mondello . . . . . . Rusty Stevens (1958–60)
Whitey Whitney . . . . Stanley Fatara
Lumpy Rutherford . . . . Frank Bank (1958–63)
Fred Rutherford . . . . Richard Deacon

Still the Beaver

The Disney Channel (1985–86)   29 Episodes

The New Leave It to Beaver

WTBS (1986–89)   76 Episodes

Cast

Beaver Cleaver . . . . Jerry Mathers
June Cleaver . . . . Barbara Billingsley
Wally Cleaver . . . . Tony Dow
Eddie Haskell . . . . Ken Osmond
Ward "Kip" Cleaver . . . . Kipp Marcus
Oliver Cleaver . . . . John Snee

Mary Ellen Cleaver . . . . Janice Kent
Kelly Cleaver . . . . Kaleena Kiff
Freddie Haskell . . . . Eric Osmond
Gert Haskell . . . . Ellen Maxted
Lumpy Rutherford . . . . Frank Bank

Orbit City

The Jetsons (1962–63, 1984–85, 1987–88)

created by Bill Hanna and Joseph Barbera

Meet George Jetson . . . Jane, his wife . . . daughter Judy . . . his boy Elroy. The Jetsons live in Orbit City, somewhere on the planet Earth, sometime in the twenty-first century. The entire city is raised above ground, so the surface of the Earth is never shown (though flying islands do occasionally pass by). Like their prehistoric cousins in the Hanna-Barbera cartoon family, the Flintstones, the Jetsons are a middle-class, all-American family. They live in the Skypad Apartments in a home that can be raised or lowered depending on the weather. Like everyone living in Orbit City, they enjoy all the modern conveniences of the future, which can be easily accessed by the press of a button.

Pressing a button is what George does for a living. He is employed as a RUDI (Referential Universal Digital Indexer) for the Spacely Space Age Sprockets Company. His two-hour, three-day work week involves pushing a RUDI button on and off. He is always trying to impress his impatient boss, Mr. Cosmo C. Spacely, who is constantly hiring and firing George. Cosmo is also fighting an endless battle against his long-time competitor, Mr. Cogswell, owner of Cogswell Cogs. They are both members of the exclusive Moon Side Country Club and are constantly trying to put each other out of business. When Cogswell

---

Orbit City at a Glance

Where to Dine:
Lunar Lunche Shoppe $
Spaceburger Drive-In $

Nightlife:
The Swivel Lounge
Cosmic Cosmo

Fun Spots:
Fun Pad Amusement Park
Laser Jack Health Club

The Jetsons, along with their maid Rosie, dog Astro, and alien pet Orbitty, settle down for some after dinner television.

The entire Jetsons clan finds traveling through Orbit City a breeze in their space car.

builds a factory alongside Spacely's, George discovers that the new building is six inches over Spacely's property. Spacely promotes George and makes his rival Cogswell walk on his hands and knees, until he discovers Spacely's building is actually six inches over on Cogswell's property.

While George is at work, his wife Jane is taking care of the house with the assistance of the mechanical maid, Rosie. Thanks to modern technology, housework and cooking are a breeze. Jane prepares meals for her family using the Food-A-Rac-A-Cycle, which allows you to make a delicious meal for four by pressing a button. When that's too much trouble, the family enjoys an entire meal in pill form.

When Jane is not trying to keep George from losing his temper, she is taking care of her two children. Ten-year-old Elroy, who is a straight-A student at Little Dipper School, is a wizard in science. Elroy's faithful dog, Astro, is a big, dumb, lovable mutt who talks (sort of) and showers George with affection, whether George likes it or not. A later addition to the Jetson family was a furry alien critter named Orbitty, which Elroy brought home from a school field trip to Mars. Judy is a typical teenager who loves boys and clothes and is up on all the latest dances, like the Swivel, the Saturn Snug, and the Mercury Melt. George is overprotective of his daughter, so when she enters a songwriting contest and wins a night out with her teen idol, rock star Jet Screamer, he follows them on their date. Jet takes Judy to the Fun Pad Amusement Park to ride the Rocket Chute, to the Spaceburger Drive-in for a bite, and then to the Swivel Lounge, where Jet introduces Judy's song, "Eep App Ork Ah-Ah" to a screaming crowd.

Nobody walks in Orbit City because moving sidewalks called "people movers" will take you from place to place. When George takes Astro out for his walk, they stand on a treadmill attached to the outside of the house. The primary mode of transportation, however, is the space car, which can conveniently fold up into a suitcase. Although the speed limit can be as high as fifteen hundred miles per hour,

George still runs into traffic on the way home. Jane Jetson, who is not so skilled behind the wheel, does very little driving. When the Jetsons go shopping for a new car at Molecular Motors, they are disappointed that the Supersonic Suburbanite they have their eye on is too expensive, so they have to stick with the

Did You Know?

When *The Jetsons* debuted in prime time during the 1962–63 season, it faired poorly in the ratings. The series found an audience when it was rerun on Saturday mornings. Over the years it has been on each of the three major networks. In the mid-1980s, forty-one new episodes were added to the original twenty-four to make the series more viable for syndication.

The Jetsons starred in two feature films. In the 1987 made-for-TV film *The Jetsons Meet the Flintstones,* the Flintstones and the Rubbles travel to the future, while the Jetsons are transported back to the Stone Age. In *Jetsons: The Movie* (1990), George becomes the managing director of a subsidiary of Spacely Space Sprockets on another planet.

Penny Singleton, the voice of Jane Jetson, played Blondie in a series of motion picture feature comedies in the 1930s and '40s based on the Chic Young comic strip.

same model. George accidentally drives off the lot with the wrong car, which unfortunately belongs to an escaped convict named Knuckles Nuclear.

The Jetsons have not always been happy living in the big city. At one point they decided to move to the moon, where a real estate broker promised plenty of room. Unfortunately, the broker has been making the same promise to everyone. When the moon becomes overcrowded, the Jetsons realize they might as well be living back in Orbit City.

Like their prehistoric counterparts, the Flintstones, the Jetsons enjoy getting out of town for a vacation. George travels on a business trip to Las Venus,

Meet George Jetson....Jane, his wife...daughter Judy...his boy Elroy.

the futuristic version of Las Vegas. They stay at the Supersonic Sands where they play the slots and see Dean Martian's stage show. The family has also traveled to Pleasure Planet to see a flea circus. The fleas are not being treated well by their owner, so they hop onto

Astro, who takes them back home. Another popular vacation spot is Fantasy Planet, a futuristic version of Fantasy Island, where everyone's dream can come true. George becomes the head of his own company, Jane is waited on hand and foot by servants, Judy becomes the most popular girl in the galaxy, and Elroy becomes a superhero. All four discover there are drawbacks to getting your wish granted.

RECOMMENDED VIEWING

To get a feel for life in Orbit City, the following episodes are recommended:

"Rosie the Robot"
Jane takes advantage of a one-day trial offer and brings home a used robot maid named Rosie. When George brings Mr. Spacely home for dinner, his boss meets the maid and realizes he has been paying George too much. Fortunately, Mr. Spacely has a change of heart and George decides to let Rosie stay to take care of his family. Original airdate: 9/23/62

"A Date With Jet Screamer"
Judy wins a date with pop star Jet Screamer. When George fails to prevent his daughter from winning the contest, he decides to act as a chaperone on the date without letting Judy know it. Original airdate: 9/30/62

"The Coming of Astro"
Elroy finds a dog and brings him home. Everyone in the family is happy to have Astro to protect the family—except George. He insists on having an electronic dog and insists the two compete to decide which dog stays and which one goes. Original airdate: 10/21/62

The Jetsons

Premiere Airdate: September 23, 1962
ABC (1962–63)   24 Episodes

Syndicated (1984–85, 1987–88)   41 Episodes

Original Voices

George Jetson	George O'Hanlon	Astro	Don Messick
Jane Jetson	Penny Singleton	Cosmo C. Spacely	Mel Blanc
Judy Jetson	Janet Waldo	Rosie and Stella Spacely	Jean Vander Pyl
Elroy Jetson	Daws Butler		

Peyton Place's town square provides the ideal setting for a group photo (clockwise from top): Dr. Michael Rossi (Ed Nelson), Norman Harrington (Christopher Connelly), Rodney Harrington (Ryan O'Neal), Betty Anderson (Barbara Parkins), Allison Mackenzie (Mia Farrow), and Eliot Carson (Tim O'Connor).

Peyton Place

Peyton Place (1964–69)

Created by Paul Monash

Based on the novel by Grace Metalious

Return to Peyton Place (1972–74)

Produced by Don Wallace and George Paris

Peyton Place, a small New England town located ninety miles from Boston, is the setting of one of the memorable dramatic series of the 1960s. It was also the setting of Grace Metalious' best-selling novel, which served as the basis of the TV show and a big screen adaptation in 1957 starring Lana Turner as heroine Constance Mackenzie. It was actually 20th Century Fox, the studio that produced the film, that realized the town of Peyton Place provided the perfect setting for a prime-time television series.

This picturesque coastal town may seem quaint and serene on the outside, but the lives of its residents are far from quiet and ordinary. Everyone who lives in or is just passing through Peyton is either battling a personal demon, guarding a family secret, or engaging in some form of criminal activity.

To understand Peyton Place is to understand the people who live there. Over fifty characters were introduced during the series'

Peyton Place at a Glance

Where to Stay:
   The Colonial Post Inn $$

Where to Dine:
   Peyton Pharmacy $

Nightlife:
   The Shoreline Club $$
   Ada Jacks' Tavern $

Local Newspaper:
   The Clarion

Peyton Place is a historic New England town founded in 1650.

five year run and their relationships are complex. But to simplify matters, it's best to begin with the town's namesake—the Peyton family.

Peyton Place was founded in 1650 (the town celebrated its 314th birthday in 1964 with a big parade). Martin Peyton, the patriarch of the Peyton family and the richest man in town, is owner of the town's main industry, the Peyton Mill, and most of the other businesses in town. He also sits on the Board of Trustees of Peyton General Hospital and lives in the largest house in town, the Peyton mansion.

All of the secrets that plague the town can either be directly or indirectly traced back to him. Martin Peyton has one daughter, Catherine, who gave birth to two sons, Norman and Rodney Harrington. The boys were ignored by their mother, so they were raised by their father, Leslie Harrington, who manages the family mill. Catherine's lack of interest in her children didn't prevent her from later giving birth to illegitimate twins, Steven and Ann, whose father, Brian Cord, was married at the time to his wife Hannah. When the twins were born, Catherine gave them up. Brian and the childless Hannah separated and each took one of the children: Ann went to live with her father, while Hannah agreed to raise Steven. Hannah also became Martin Peyton's personal assistant, but she kept the fact that Steven's mother was Catherine a secret.

The town of Peyton Place is basically a large square with a park in the center. The park has a pillory, which was used in the colonial days to lock up "sinful" women. Surrounding the town square are various shops and businesses, including *The Clarion*, the local newspaper for which the town space case, teenager Allison Mackenzie, wrote before her disappearance, and the Peyton courthouse, where the town's district attorney, John Fowler, is kept busy by all the murder, deceit, and treachery. When visitors

stroll around the square, they can drop in and chat with Eli Carson, the kind old coot who runs the chandlery; Constance Mackenzie, Allison's mother and owner of the local bookstore; Rodney Harrington, who is usually fixing a car in the Shoreline Garage; and Rita Jacks, who is busy behind the counter at Peyton Pharmacy. Rita's mother is proprietor of Ada Jacks' Tavern, the local joint complete with a jukebox and

There's never a dull moment in Peyton Place for resident teenagers Rodney Harrington (Ryan O'Neal), Allison Mackenzie (Mia Farrow), and Betty Anderson (Barbara Parkins).

thirsty fishermen who stop in for a beer and a brawl when they get off their boats. Practicing at the piano is Chris Webber, who was blinded by a fall when his bad boy brother Lee pushed him off Sailor's Bluff when they were children. Lee was also responsible, but never punished, for the murder of Ann Howard, whom he also pushed off a cliff. Chris can also be heard playing piano at Peyton's most posh night spot, the Shoreline Country Club.

Three years after the series' five-year run, *Peyton Place* was revived as a daytime series on NBC. Three members of the original cast, Patricia Morrow, Evelyn Scott, and Frank Ferguson, reprised their roles. Martin Peyton, who had died in the original series, was brought back to life and Allison Mackenzie, whose disappearance was never explained, was back in town. The revival was canceled after two years, but the story con-

Peyton Place in Gilmanton, New Hampshire

This small New England community in the Lakes region of New Hampshire was the home of *Peyton Place* author Grace Metalious. When the best-seller was published in 1965, the residents of Gilmanton were not pleased with how the author depicted her hometown. Metalious, who was a heavy drinker, died in 1964 at the age of thirty-nine from a liver-related illness. Her grave is in the Smith Meeting House cemetery on Smith Meeting House Road.

Did You Know?

Peyton Place launched the careers of two of the biggest film stars of the late 1960s and early 1970s, Mia Farrow and Ryan O'Neal. The show also featured several up-and-coming film and television stars, including Gena Rowlands, Emmy-winner Lee Grant, Leslie Nielsen, Mariette Hartley, David Canary, Leigh Taylor-Young, Ruby Dee, and Glynn Turman.

Peyton Place was canceled in 1969 before it resolved a major plotline. In the final episode, Dr. Michael Rossi is awaiting trial for the murder of Fred Russell.

The series peaked in popularity during its first season, when it was on twice a week (Tuesdays and Thursday evenings). In October 1965, ABC added a third night, but as ratings began to decline, the network cut the series back to one night.

The outdoor set for *Peyton Place* was built on a studio lot. The producers went to great lengths to recreate a New England town.

There are no episodes of *Peyton Place* available on tape.

tinued in two television movies, *Murder in Peyton Place* (1977), which focused on the murders of Allison Mackenzie and Rodney Harrington, and *Peyton Place: The Next Generation* (1985), in which Allison's daughter Megan arrived in Peyton Place.

Peyton Place

Premiere Airdate: September 15, 1964
ABC   514 Episodes

Cast

Constance Mackenzie Carson
       Dorothy Malone (1964–68)
Allison Mackenzie . . . . . . Mia Farrow (1964–69)
Rodney Harrington . . . . Ryan O'Neal
Betty Anderson . . . . Barbara Parkins
Norman Harrington . . . . . . Christopher Connelly

Rita Jacks . . . . Patricia Morrow
Martin Peyton . . . . George Macready
Lee Webbe . . . . Steven Oliver (1966–68)
Chris Webber . . . . Gary Haynes (1966–67)
Hannah Cord . . . . Ruth Warrick (1965–67)

Return to Peyton Place

Premiere Airdate: April 3, 1972
NBC   50 Episodes

Cast

Constance Mackenzie
       . . . . Bette Ackerman (1972)
       . . . . Susan Brown (1972–74)
Allison Mackenzie . . Katherine Glass (1972–73)
       . . . . Pamela Shoop (1973–74)
Rodney Harrington . . . . . Laurence Casey (1972)
       . . . . Yale Summers (1972–74)

Betty Anderson Harrington
       . . . . Julie Parrish (1972–73)
       . . . . Lynn Loring (1973–74)
Norman Harrington . . . . Ron Russell
Rita Jacks Harrington . . . . Patricia Morrow
Hannah Cord . . . . Mary K. Welles
Martin Peyton . . . . John Hoyt (1972–73)

In the 1980s, Officer Frisco Jones (Jack Wagner) and Police Commissioner Robert Scorpio (Tristan Rogers) worked together to control the mob's operations along the docks of the Port Charles River.

Port Charles, New York

General Hospital (1963–Present)

Created by Frank and Doris Hursley

Port Charles (1997–Present)

Created by Richard and Carolyn Culliton

The city of Port Charles, founded in 1781, is located in upstate New York. The town serves as the setting for the long-running daytime soap opera *General Hospital* and its recent spinoff *Port Charles*. When *General Hospital* debuted in 1963, the series focused exclusively on the professional and personal lives of the doctors, nurses, and patients of a large private hospital. The plotlines revolved around malpractice suits, love affairs, divorce, pregnancy, and cancer.

Although the major characters would remain directly or indirectly connected to the hospital, the stories over the years began to focus less on the hospital and more on the town of Port Charles. When poor ratings threatened to cancel the soap in the late 1970s, producer Gloria Monty breathed new life into the show by introducing younger characters, including the most popular couple in soap opera history, Luke and Laura

Kelly's Diner is a popular eating spot for the locals, including Laura Templeton (Janine Turner) and Blackie Parrish (John Stamos).

Spencer. When daytime's supercouple tied the knot on November 16 and 17, 1981, a record-breaking thirty million viewers tuned in.

Port Charles is a medium-sized city that seems to have everything—industry, culture, a major university, a top-notch medical center, and so on. The city has a small-town feel to it. Families still enjoy picnics in the town park, while residents will go down to the waterfront to have lunch at Kelly's Diner, where they are sure to run into someone they know. Yet Port Charles has continually been the site of scandals, intrigue, and danger, no doubt because it is a port city. Even though it rests on a river and not the Atlantic Ocean, it still seems to attract members of the international community of madmen, spies, and just plain bad guys.

Port Charles is infested with organized crime and over the years it has been difficult for the police department to keep it under control. In fact, in 1986, the police co-chief Burt Ramsey turned out to be the head of a mob ring known only as Mr. Big. The mob first took interest in Port Charles in the late 1970s, when Frank Smith used the popular night spot, the Campus Disco, for his money-laundering operation. When Smith put a contract out on Laura after she overheard information about his operations, Luke, who was working for Smith, fled Port Charles with her. Smith created trouble for the Spencers for sixteen years, until Luke finally gunned him down in a graveyard in Puerto Rico in 1994.

In the late 1980s, the Jerome crime family controlled Port Charles, although the inner conflicts between father Victor, daughter Olivia, and son Julian would lead to their eventual downfall. Victor experienced an untimely death when he reacted to Lucy Coe's rejection of his love by swallowing a heart-shaped pendant with the engraving "Victor and Lucy Forever." When Olivia is shot by Julian, who was gunned down himself by Duke Lavery, the Jeromes' reign of terror came to an end.

More recently, Sonny Corinthos, a mobster with a conscience, took over as head of the Port Charles crime syndicate. Corinthos' operation was initially bankrolled by none other than Frank Smith's son, Damian. Sonny's reign as Port Charles public enemy number one has brought nothing but tragedy to those around him, including the death of his wife Lily and their unborn child. They were killed by a car bomb planted by Lily's own father, who was trying to bump off Sonny. Both Sonny and his protégé, Jason Morgan (a.k.a. Quartermaine), who took over the organization in Sonny's absence, continue to battle their nemesis, Moreno.

Port Charles has overcome a series of tragedies and near tragedies. The city was devastated by a hurricane in 1977 and a major earthquake (no doubt the first in up-state New York) in 1991. The hospital was placed under quarantine in 1979 due to an outbreak of Lassa Fever. More recently, a strain of flu virus nearly killed members of the Port Charles family when a contaminated vial of experimental drug DL56 broke in Mario's restaurant. Luckily, members of the General Hospital staff were able to create a vaccine. The entire city was almost turned into a popsicle when Mikkos Cassadine created a weather machine that produced carbonic, a substance that he planned to use to control the world's weather. Luckily, Luke was able to shut down the machine by figuring out the computer password ("Ice Princess"), thereby saving the entire world. Luke received helped during the Ice Princess caper (the world's largest uncut diamond) from Robert Scorpio, a member of the WSB (World Security Bureau) who would have a strong presence in Port Charles in the years to follow.

In between all the devastation and intrigue, the residents of Port Charles know how to relax and have a good time. The two favorite watering holes are Luke's Club and the Outback, which is owned by current police commissioner Mac Scorpio. Both clubs have attracted some serious talent. Luke celebrated his opening with a live performance by B.B. King. The Outback featured local talent over the years, including Miguel Morez (pop singer Ricky Martin), Mary Mae Ward (blues singer Rosalind Cash), and Eddie Maine (a.k.a. Ned Ashton), and the Idle Rich. The club has also played host to singer Melissa Manchester.

When Port Charles residents have food on their mind, they can enjoy the fine cuisine at the Port Charles Hotel, owned by the Quartermaine family. For down-home cooking, there's the always reliable Kelly's Diner, which also doubles as a boarding-house. Located by the waterfront, Kelly's is an institution in Port Charles. The diner's current owner, Luke, worked there in 1980. When the former owner, his beloved Aunt Ruby, died in January 1998, Luke decided to reopen the diner's doors and allow Tammy, a former prostitute, to run the diner. The waterfront is a rough neighborhood, but if you don't mind the occasional mob shootout or warehouse fire, it's definitely worth the trip down to Kelly's for a quick bite.

The residents of Port Charles are a mixture of the super-rich and working-class folks. The wealthiest family in town (and one of the richest in New York State) are the Quartermaines, who reside in a mansion at 66 Harbour View Road. Patriarch Edward Quartermaine relocated his family to Port Charles from Southampton when his son, Dr. Alan Quartermaine, moved to town. Edward is the founder of ELQ, a conglomerate with holdings around the world. Many bargains have been struck among Port Charles' wealthier citizens over the ownership of ELQ stock. The company has experienced some hard times, such as when one of their boats, the SS *Tracy,* was sabotaged and exploded and sank in Port Charles Harbor.

There are several other companies headquartered in Port Charles, including two cosmetic companies: Deception, owned by Lucy Coe, and Jax Cosmetics, which is

Two of Port Charles' most notorious citizens—Luke Spencer (Tony Geary) and Helena Cassadine (Elizabeth Taylor).

part of Jax Enterprises. The latter is owned by the rich and handsome Jasper Jax, whose family travels in the same international business circles as the Quartermaines. Smitten with the late Brenda Barrett, Jax took up residence in Port Charles in the penthouse suite of the Port Charles Hotel.

The biggest social event in Port Charles is the annual Nurse's Ball, which benefits AIDS research in memory of Stone Cates, who died of the disease in 1995. The ball includes a talent show featuring the residents of Port Charles performing musical and comedy numbers, culminating each year with co-chairperson and host Lucy Coe ending up on stage in her underwear. The ball ended tragically in 1998 when Dr. Jake Marshak's body was found hanging backstage from the rafters. He was the victim of the General Hospital killer, who was murdering members of the hospital staff in a pattern that mirrored the events in Kevin Collins' mystery novel, *General Homicide*. The killer was revealed to be Julie Devlin, who was under the control of Greg Cooper, a vengeful medical student who was not admitted into the hospital's intern program.

Greg Cooper is not the only one to wreak havoc in Port Charles. Helena Cassadine, the vengeful matriarch of a prestigious Greek family, blames Luke and Laura for her son Mikko's death. Laura was held captive by Helena and during that time she had a son, Nicholas, who now lives in Windemere, the Cassadine estate located on Spoon Island. Windemere is a Gothic house (Luke often refers to it as "Dracula's Castle"), which provides the perfect setting for the evil and treachery surrounding the Cassadine dynasty.

RECOMMENDED VIEWING

Daytime's Greatest Weddings: General Hospital.

General Hospital

Premiere Airdate: April 1, 1963
ABC

Cast

Dr. Alan Quartermaine . . . . Stuart Damon
Bobbie Spencer . . . . Jacqueline Zeman
Luke Spencer . . . . Tony Geary
Laura Spencer . . . . Genie Francis
Edward Quartermaine
. . . . . . John Ingle (1993–Present)
. . . . David Lewis (1978–93)
Lila Quartermaine . . . Anna Lee (1978–Present)
. . . . Meg Wylie (1994)
Ned Ashton . . . . . . Wally Kurth (1991–Present)
. . Kurt Robin McKinney (1988–91)

Dr. Monica Quartermaine
. Leslie Charleson (1977–Present)
. . . . Patsy Rahn (1976–77)
Sonny Corinthos . . . . Maurice Bernard
A.J. Quartermaine
. . . . Billy Warlock (1997–Present)
. . . . Sean Kanan (1993–97)
Felicia Scorpio . . . . Kristina Wagner
Mac Scorpio . . . . John J. York

Port Charles

Premiere Airdate: June 1, 1997
ABC

Cast

Audrey Hardy . . . . Rachel Ames
Dr. Gail Baldwin . . . . Susan Brown
Lucy Coe . . . . Lynn Herring
Dr. Kevin Collins . . . . Jon Lindstrom
Mary Scanlon . . . . Pat Crowley

Mike Corbin . . . . Ron Hale
Dr. Eve Lambert . . . . Julie Pinson
Scott Baldwin . . . . Kin Shriner
Serena Baldwin . . . . Carly Schroeder

In the pursuit of eternal love—Hope (Kristian Alfonso) and Bo (Peter Reckell).

Salem

Days of Our Lives (1965–Present)

Created by Ted and Betty Corday

Salem at a Glance

Where to Stay:
>   The Continental Hotel $$$
>   Salem Inn $$

Where to Dine:
>   The Penthouse Grille $$$
>   Chez Vous $$$
>   The Tuscany $$$
>   Brady Pub $$
>   Johnny Angel's $

Nightlife:
>   The Blue Note
>   The Salem Club

Where to Shop:
>   Salem Place Mall
>   Barron's Department Store

Local Newspapers:
>   *The Salem Chronicle*
>   *The Spectator*
>   *The Salem Tribune*
>   *The Intruder*

Salem, a small, midwestern town, is the setting of this long-running soap opera, which focuses on the trials and tribulations of two Salem families, the Hortons and the Bradys. The Hortons are an upper middle-class family headed by matriarch Alice, whose husband Tom was chief of staff of Salem University Medical Center until his death in 1994. Tom and Alice had five children: Tom "Tommy" Horton Jr.; his twin sister Addie, who died in 1974; Micky Horton, an attorney; Bill Horton, a surgeon; and Marie Horton, a nurse. The Bradys, a large working-class Irish family, is headed by Shawn and Caroline Brady, who spend most of their time tending Brady's Pub. They raised four children—Bo, Kim, Kayla, and Roman, whose biological father is Victor Kiriakis.

Salem is located in Salem County, which borders Jones County on the east and Goodhue County on the west. The exact location of Salem is unknown, although it is located in a tri-state area close to a large midwestern city, perhaps Cleveland or Chicago (the consensus among viewers is that Salem is in Illi-

The first couple of Salem—the late Dr. Tom Horton (Macdonald Carey) and Alice Horton (Frances Reid).

nois). The call letters of the local TV station, WGTB-TV (formerly WATB), begin with a "W," which suggests that Salem is located east of the Mississippi. The town sits near a large unnamed lake (one of the Great Lakes?) which is connected to an unnamed river which flows through Salem County. Visitors can arrive by airplane into Salem In-ternational Airport (on National or Sun West Airline) or by train into Salem Central Train Station.

Salem is a town that has everything. There are parks, museums, churches, health clubs, and a civic center. There is a community college as well as Salem University, which is where the hospital is located.

The hospital is part of the Salem University Medical Center, which includes an emergency center, a mental health clinic, a fertility clinic, a trauma center, and The Tom Horton Youth Center. Under the leadership of Commissioner Samuels and Commander Abe Carter, Salem also has a top-notch police department. Considering Salem's crime rate, it's not surprising the Salem police department, fire department, and the state penitentiary are kept extremely busy.

First-time visitors to Salem will want to stay at the Salem Inn (4300 Washington Avenue). The inn's owner, Alex Marshall, set it on fire in 1987 to collection the insurance money. The renovation that followed managed to retain the old-fashioned charm of the original building. It contains a restaurant and lounge as well as a banquet hall and meeting rooms for conferences. More luxurious accommodations are available at the Continental Hotel, which has a restaurant and bar frequented by Salem's wealthier residents.

Salem visitors have an even wider choice of restaurants. The most expensive restaurants in town are the Penthouse Grille, which sits at the top of the Titan Publishing building; the more formal Chez Vous, located near Salem Place; and Salem's newest restaurant, the Tuscany. For more down-home cooking, there's the Brady Pub at 48 Riber Street. Known for its clam chowder, this is the place to be on St. Patrick's Day.

The locals also enjoy burgers and fries at Johnny Angel's and coffee and good conversation in the Java Café, which are both located in the Salem Place Mall. The mall has become the shopping hub of Salem since it opened its doors in 1992. The complex houses a department store, clothing stores, an antique store, a hair salon, and a cinema with three screens.

There are several corporations with holdings in Salem, though the longest battle has been waged between Kate Roberts and her nemesis, Vivian Kiriakis, over the control of Titan Publishing. Located in a high-rise building at 14 Salem Circle, Titan publishes several publications including *Bella Magazine,* a fashion magazine; *The Spectator,* a tabloid newspaper; and *Focus, Sports Today,* and *City Style.* The Titan conglomerate shares its complex with the Titan Health Club, Countess Wilhemina Cosmetics, and the Penthouse Grille.

Although Salem seems quite peaceful on the surface, the town has been terrorized over the years by various serial killers and rapists. In 1981, the Salem Strangler, Jake Kositchek, killed his first victim. Obsessed with Angel, one of Jessica Blake's personalities, Jake went over the edge when poor Jessica, who was suffering from multiple personality disorder, fell apart. He began strangling Salem women and threatening Dr. Marlena Evans through letters and phone calls to her radio show. He also left Marlena a present in her apartment—a doll with a broken neck hanging from a silk scarf. When Jake broke into Marlena's apartment to kill her, he mistakenly murdered her twin sister, Samantha. When he realized his mistake, he returned to Marlena's apartment. Jake was shot to death when a gun went off during a struggle with Roman Brady.

A similar wave of murders occurred in 1983 when a madman, who became known as the Salem Slasher, poisoned and stabbed his victims and left a raven feather in their hands. Among his victims were Renee Dumonde, nurse Kelly Chase, Trista Evans Bradford, Letitia Bradford, and several hookers. The killer was Andre DiMera, who, working with Stefano, had had plastic surgery to resemble his cousin Tony and wore a mask of Roman Brady when committing the murders. The real Roman managed to clear his name by faking his own death and, once again, apprehend the killer.

The wave of terror continued in 1986 when a string of rapes occurred in the hospital and on the waterfront. Ian Griffith, who became obsessed with Melissa Anderson, terrorized the hospital. When his attempt to rape her failed, she was able to identify him and turn him in to the police. Another stalker, who preyed on women in 1994, turned out to be a Salem University undergraduate, Alan Harris, who was obsessed with Carrie Brady. Alan raped Sami Brady and held both sisters at gunpoint. When Alan was found not guilty for his crime, Sami took the law into her own hands and shot Alan in the groin.

The waterfront was the location of another series of killings committed in 1987 and 1988 by Harper Deveraux, who became known as the Riverfront Knifer. As an act of revenge against all the women who wronged him, Harper began stabbing women, mostly prostitutes. Kayla Brady managed to survive the attack, but Deveraux left her deaf and mute. He also attacked Kayla's pregnant sister, Kimberly, who lost her baby. Luckily, Steve Johnson came to the rescue. Harper managed to break out of prison, but he was once again apprehended (but not before he

Did You Know?

"Like sands through the hourglass, so are the days of our lives." The voice you hear belongs to the late MacDonald Carey, who played Dr. Tom Horton from 1965 until his death in 1994. The real hourglass used in the original introduction has been replaced by an electronically generated image.

Days of Our Lives was the first soap opera to be broadcast in color.

Days is a family affair. The show's producers, Ted and Betty Corday, were succeeded by their son, the show's current producer, Ken Corday.

Some of the stars who appeared on *Days* include Pamela Anderson, Christina Applegate (at the age of three months), Cindy Crawford, Farrah Fawcett, Vivica Fox, Mary Frann, French Stewart, and Joan Van Ark.

Lovers on and off-screen—Doug (Bill Hayes) and Julie (Susan Seaforth Hayes).

once again took Kayla prisoner in the Riverfront Clinic).

Evil comes to Salem in many forms. Since the rich, powerful, and mysterious Stefano arrived in town in 1982, Salem has never been the same. Stefano lives in the DiMera mansion (430 Lakeview Drive), which is filled with secret rooms where he has held his many captives. Stefano is the kidnapping king of Salem. He has kidnapped Marlena Evans three times and almost every member of the Brady family. He has practiced mind control over several of Salem's residents, including John Black, Laura Horton, Vivian Alamain, Hope Brady, and the object of his affection, Marlena. He has fathered and adopted a long list of children and has managed to cheat death numerous times. Known as "The Phoenix" because of his ability to continually come back from the dead, he has survived a stroke, a shooting, a plane crash, and numerous explosions.

The devil himself even made an appearance in the appropriately named Salem when Marlena was possessed. She became the "Desecrator" and wreaked havoc on Salem by setting the town Christmas tree on fire as well as the church where Kristen and Tony DiMera exchanged their wedding vows. The Desecrator caused more problems by sending a series of plagues over Salem, including a heat wave, a drought, and bees. Fortunately, Marlena was saved when Father John Black successfully performed an exorcism.

Another menace to the community is Salem's leading businessman, Victor Kiriakis, who lives in the family mansion at 13201 Glen Oaks Drive. As head of Salem's crime syndicate, Victor financed Salem's drug and pornography ring, committed blackmail, arranged a jail break, drugged his nephew, and framed Kayla Johnson for murder.

Victor has been in the center of a power struggle between Kate Roberts and Vivian Alamain. When Kate went to a fertility clinic to have Victor's child, Vivian switched her embryo with Kate's. If that wasn't enough, Vivian then tricked Victor into marrying her when she stood in for Kate during Victor and Kate's wedding rehearsal!

In Salem, that's just business as usual.

Days of Our Lives

Premiere Airdate: November 8, 1965
NBC

Cast

Marlena Brady.................. Deidre Hall
John Black................. Drake Hogestyn
Stefano DiMera .... Joseph Mascolo
Caroline Brady .... Peggy McCay
Bo Brady..................... Peter Reckell
Roman Brady.................. Josh Taylor
Hope Brady .... Kristian Alfonso
Billie Brady............... Jamie Lyn Bauer
Alice Horton .... Frances Reid

Maggie Horton .... Suzanne Rogers
Kate Kirakis .... Lauren Koslow
Vivian Alamain................. Louise Sorel
Sami Brady .... Alison Sweeny
Austin Reed .... Austin Peck
Lucas Roberts................. Bryan Dattilo
Nancy Wesley............... Patrika Darbo
Craig Wesley .... Kevin Spirtas

A typical Springfield family, The Simpsons—Homer and Marge and their
children, Lisa, Bart, and Maggie.

Springfield

The Simpsons (1989–Present)

Created by Matt Groening

Springfield at a Glance

Town Motto:
"A Noble Spirit Embiggens the Smallest Man"

Official Song:
"Embiggen the Soul"

Official Tree: Lemon Tree

Where to Stay:
The Springfield Palace Hotel $$$
The Happy Earwig Hotel $$
Aphrodite Inn $$
Ye Olde Off-Ramp Inn $$
Sleep-Eazy Motel $

Where to Dine:
The Gilded Truffle $$$
The Springfield Revolving Restaurant $$$
The Frying Dutchman $$
Planet Hype $$
Wall E. Weasel's $
Krusty Burger $

Favorite Hangout:
Moe's Tavern

Where to Shop:
Hailstone's Department Store
South Street Squidport

Springfield is the home of *The Simpsons,* the longest-running prime-time animated series. Homer J. Simpson, wife Marge Bouvier Simpson, son Bart J., and daughters Lisa and Maggie reside in the small suburban city at 742 Evergreen Terrace. The name of the town is the same as the hometown of another popular television family, the Andersons, from the 1950s comedy *Father Knows Best.* But Homer Simpson is no Jim Anderson and the Springfield of the 1990s bears no resemblance to the squeaky clean, crime-free town of the 1950s. The Springfield of today is a postmodern version of an all-American town, where green parks and swimming holes have been replaced by fast-food restaurants, shopping malls, and a nuclear power plant.

The actual location of Springfield is unknown, though the writers have given us hundreds of clues, most of which are contradictory. The town is bordered by a body of water (complete with a port, boardwalk, and lighthouse), yet the desert is only a bus ride away. The call letters of the local radio and television stations begin with K and the town appears to be on Pacific or Mountain time, suggesting that it's west of the Missis-

A replica of the Simpson's house in Henderson, Nevada was the grand prize in a 1997 contest won by Mrs. Barbara Howard of Richmond, Kentucky.

sippi, and far enough north to get snow in the winter. The state initials on Homer's driver's license are NT, which leads many Simpson trivia fans to believe Springfield is in the fictional state of North Takoma.

Springfield was founded in the 1796 by a frontiersman named Jebediah Obediah Zachariah Jebediah Springfield, who led a group of pioneers from Maryland. A statue of the town's founder, standing on a bear carcass, sits in the town square (Bart created chaos in the town when he sawed the head off the statue). Springfield's rival town, Shelbyville, was founded by Jebediah's former partner, Shelbyville Manhattan. The duo parted ways over a disagreement about whether cousins should be allowed to marry, a concept Jebediah opposed.

While researching her essay on Jebediah at the Springfield Historical Society for the town's bicentennial, Lisa discovered a confession written by Springfield's founding father on his deathbed. Jebediah admitted he was really a pirate named Hans Sprungfield who had a prosthetic tongue made of silver when his real tongue was bitten off by a Turk in a fight. He was a vicious man who tried to kill George Washington and stole the bottom of his portrait (on which he wrote his last confession). When Jebediah's body was exhumed, there was no silver tongue, but with a little help from Washington's ghost, Lisa realized the town historian, Mr. Hurlbut, stole the tongue. Because of all the good it has brought to Springfield, Lisa agreed to let the myth of Jebediah live on.

Jebediah was also believed to be the founder of a Springfield local holiday known as Whacking Day. According to legend, the townspeople gathered on May 10, 1775, to drive the snakes out of the town square and club them to death. Bart and Lisa put an end to the barbaric ritual of slaughtering the snakes by luring all the snakes to safety in their house and informing the town that Whacking Day does not date back to the town's forefathers, but actually started in 1924.

On the surface, Springfield does not appear to be an ideal place to live. *Newsweek* magazine dubbed Springfield "America's crud bucket," while *Time* magazine did a cover story on "Springfield, America's Worst City." In a national survey, Springfield was voted the least popular city in America, due to the city's nuclear power plant, toxic waste dump, and tire yard, in which a fire has been burning since 1966.

The mayor of Springfield is "Diamond" Joe Quimby, a Democrat whose political career has been rocked by scandal. Conservative commentator Birch Barlow once referred to him as an "illiterate, tax cheating, wife-swapping, pot smoking, spend-o-crat." ("Hey, I am no longer illiterate," was Quimby's response.) While seeking his seventh term, Quimby was challenged by Sideshow Bob, Krusty the Klown's former sidekick, who had framed Krusty for armed robbery. After Mayor Quimby granted Bob a pardon from prison, Bob decided to run for mayor on the Republican ticket. Bob won by a landslide, but Bart and Lisa exposed him for voter fraud (he stuffed the ballot box with the names of animals buried in the pet cemetery).

Other scandals in Springfield include the building of a $3 million monorail. Marge Simpson opposed the project and believed the money should be used to fix Main Street. During the opening ceremony, it was discovered that Springfield had purchased a used monorail (left over from the 1964 World's Fair), which went out of control during its inaugural run. Luckily, monorail conductor Homer managed to stop the train. The remnants of the Springfield monorail and the Central Monorail Station are still standing, a

Lisa accompanies brother Bart to the all-male Rommelwood Military Academy to learn a little discipline.

block the sun, thereby forcing all of Springfield to use the energy from his nuclear power plant. Fortunately, little Maggie Simpson aborted the plan by accidentally shooting Mr. Burns.

From an economic standpoint, industry is thriving in Springfield. The city is an exporter of melted hog fat, fake vomit, sulfur, and galoshes. There is also a booming food industry, which includes crackers, caramel, peanuts, "Ah, Fudge" chocolate, and Duff Beer. Homer is employed at the Springfield Nuclear Power Plant and is a member of the International Brotherhood of Jazz Dancers, Pastry Chefs, and Nuclear Technicians Local 643. The nuclear power plant is part of BurnsoDyne, which also includes a casino, recycling center, blood bank, construction company, ticket master, and a chain of nursing homes.

Springfield is a shopper's paradise. The Springfield Harbor has been renovated into a shopping district, the South Street Squidport, which boasts a large selection of upscale specialty chain stores, including It's a Wonderful Knife (a wide selection of cut-

painful reminder of a very expensive disaster. Another project that luckily did not get beyond the planning stages was J. Montgomery Burns' attempt to build a device to lery), Malaria Zone (for jungle adventurers), and Turban Outfitters. Springfield shoppers also love to browse at the International House of Answering Machines, the Potholder Barn, Bloodbath and Beyond Gun Shop (for all your firepower needs), and the Springfield Harmonica Shop. There's also the Leftorium, which boasts to have "everything for the left-handed man, woman, and child."

As long as nutrition is not a priority, there are plenty of dining options in Springfield to satiate the heartiest of appetites. Fast-food lovers will want to check out Gulp-N-Blow; Taco Mat, which offers a hundred tacos for a hundred dollars; and Bart's favorite, Krusty Burger. Meat eaters like Homer have a wide selection of meateries, including Greasy Joe's Bottomless Bar-B-Q Pit; P. Piggly Hogswine Super Smorg; and the Singing Sirloin, Home of Ballads and Salads. For more international fare, try Tanen's Fatty Meats, located in Springfield's Jewish section in the Lower East Side; Chez Guevara—Palacio de Danza Cubana, which has the best mambo music in Springfield; Two Guys from Kabul, the only Pakistanian restaurant in town; and Happy Sumo, a Japanese restaurant and karaoke bar. For a meal that's just plain fun, there's Wall E. Weasel's ("we cram fun down your throats") and Planet Hype, where the entire menu was approved by the secretary of one of its co-owners, action film star Rainer Wolfcastle. For a terrific view of Springfield while you dine, experience the Springfield Re-volving Restaurant (as Principal Skinner says, "Food tastes better when you're revolving"). If there's room for more, dig into a Splittsville Ice Cream Sundae or one of the 5600 flavors at Phineas Q. Butterfat's Ice Cream Parlor.

To keep their minds off the fact they live in Springfield, both residents and tourists

Did You Know?

Creator Matt Groening named Marge and Homer Simpson after his own parents. Lisa and Maggie are the names of his younger sisters.

There are many stories surrounding the origins of *The Simpsons*. Jim Brooks, executive producer of *The Tracy Ullman Show*, supposedly got the idea of hiring Matt Groening from the "Life is Hell" poster (Groening's original strip) on his wall. Groening had the original idea for *The Simpsons* while he was sitting outside of Brooks' office waiting for a meeting.

In 1997, a sixty-three-year-old great-grandmother from Kentucky won a contest sponsored by the Pepsi-Cola Company. First prize was a 2200 square foot, four-bedroom house that is identical to the Simpson's house. It is now a tourist attraction outside of Las Vegas in Henderson, Nevada.

can visit one of the many local attractions. For a trip back in time, there's Olde Springfield Towne, where visitors can stick their heads into a real wooden stock. Prehistoric Springfield is one display at the Springfield Natural History Museum (check out the static electricity exhibit) and the nearby Springfield Tar Pits (free bucket of tar with every admission). Free food and drink samples are also offered at the Ah, Fudge Factory; Duff Brewery; and for those on the wagon, Mt. Swartzwedler Historic Cider Mill, where an informed tour guide will educate the visitors who manage to stay awake on the art of making cider.

Nature lovers will want to explore Springfield's gorges and parks, including Springfield Gorge, the third most beautiful gorge in the state, over which Homer made his famous (and unsuccessful) skateboard jump. For a taste of the great outdoors, there's water sports on Lake Springfield (formerly CessHole 17a) and nature walks in the Springfield National Forest, which is still standing thanks to Lisa Simpson's ability to sniff out political corruption. For those who are a little more adventurous, Mount Useful offers both the novice and experienced hiker the chance to experience a real-live avalanche and interact with a mechanical Smokey the Bear in the visitors' center.

Other popular tourist attractions include Duff Gardens, Duff Beer's answer to Disneyland, featuring the Beerquarium, Beeramid, and the Beer Hall of Presidents. At Mt. Splashmore, visitors can challenge the raging water of death (overweight patrons should be careful going down the H2WHOA slide). Outside Springfield's city limits you'll find a theme park devoted to Bart Simpson's TV idols, Itchy and Scratchy. Masochists as well as fans of the most violent cartoon cat-and-mouse team on television may want to risk an afternoon of torture, explosions, searing gas pain, or unnecessary surgery at Itchy and Scratchy Land. Western lovers will want to check out Bloodbath Gulch Ghost Town, the friendliest town in the old west. Founded by prostitutes in 1849, it's complete with tumbleweeds, a saloon, and five brothels.

RECOMMENDED VIEWING

To get a feel for life in Springfield, the following episodes are recommended viewing:

"The New Kid on the Block"
Writer: Conan O'Brien
Director: Wes Archer

Bart develops a crush on his new neighbor, Laura (guest voice Sara Gilbert), who moves next door with her mother (guest voice Pamela Reed). Bart schemes to get rid of his rival for her affection, a biker named Jimbo. Meanwhile, Homer enjoys the all-you-can-eat special at the Frying Dutchman, but when the proprietor throws him out for overeating, he decides to take the restaurant owner, Captain McAlister, to court. Original airdate: 11/1/92

"$pringfield"
Writers: Bill Oakley and Josh Weinstein
Director: Wes Archer

When Springfield is hit with a recession, the town decides to jumpstart the economy by legalizing gambling. Mr. Burns builds a casino in Springfield and Homer fulfills his life-long dream of becoming a blackjack dealer. Original airdate: 12/16/93

"22 Films About Springfield"
Writers: Richard Apel, David S. Cohen,
**   Jonathan Collier, Jennifer Crittenden,**
**   Greg Daniels, Brent Forrester,**
**   Rachel Pulido, Steve Tompkins,**
**   Josh Weinstein, and Matt Groening**
Director: Jim Reardon

Twenty-two vignettes about the residents of Springfield feature Apu attending a party at Sanjays, Marge trying to get gum out of Lisa's hair, Burns and Smithers riding a bicycle built for two, Reverend Lovejoy walking his dog, and Principal Skinner having Superintendent Chalmers over for dinner. Original airdate: 4/14/96

The Simpsons

Premiere Airdate: December 17, 1989
FOX   243 Episodes as of March 19, 2000

Voices

Homer Simpson . . . . Dan Castellaneta	Mr. Burns, Ned Flanders, Smithers and others
Marge Simpson . . . . Julie Kavner	. . . . Harry Shearer
Bart Simpson . . . . Nancy Cartwright	Moe, Apu, and Chief Wiggum
Lisa Simpson . . . . Yeardley Smith	. . . . Hank Azaria

Guest Voices (A partial list)

Mr. Bergstrom, Lisa's substitute teacher . . . . Sam Etic a.k.a. Dustin Hoffman
Leon Kompowsky, who thinks he's Michael Jackson . . . . . John Jay Smith a.k.a. Michael Jackson
Dr. Zweig, Marge's therapist . . . . Anne Bancroft
Jessica Lovejoy, Bart's evil girlfriend . . . . Meryl Streep
Mindy Simmons, Homer's co-worker . . . . Michelle Pfeiffer
Allison Taylor, Lisa's rival . . . . Winona Ryder
Ringo Starr, Magic Johnson, Bob Hope, and Sting as themselves

Nothing brings a town closer together like a funeral. Gathered to lay Laura Palmer to rest are (left to right) Shelly Johnson (Mädchen Amick), Norma Jennings (Peggy Lipton), Ed Hurley (Everett McGill), Nadine Hurley (Wendy Robie), and Agent Dale Cooper (Kyle MacLachlan).

Twin Peaks, Washington

Twin Peaks (1990–91)

Created by David Lynch and Mark Frost

Life in Twin Peaks would never be the same once a young high school student named Laura Palmer was found murdered, her body wrapped in plastic on the shore of Black Lake. The investigation to find Laura's killer, led by special FBI agent Dale Cooper, became the focus of one of the most innovative prime-time television series.

Twin Peaks is set in a picturesque northwestern lumber town. Its population, according to the welcome sign which greets visitors as they drive into town, is 51,201 (this number would decrease significantly during the series). The town is located in the northeast corner of Washington State. In the series pilot, Agent Cooper identifies the town's location as five miles south of the Canadian border and twelve miles west of the state line. Director David Lynch (*Blue Velvet, Wild at Heart*) and co-creator Mark Frost take some liberties with the state's geography because Twin Peaks appears to be in the Cascade Mountains (the actual location used for the series), which are located in the western portion of the state.

The town was originally a settlement inhabited by trappers, thieves, and rogues, until the first lumber mill was built by Janes and Unguin Packard in the late 1890s. A second mill was built by Rudolph Martell

---

Twin Peaks at a Glance

Where to Stay:
  Great Northern Hotel $$$
  Timber Falls Motel $$

Where to Dine:
  Timber Room at the Great
    Northern $$$
  Lamplighter Inn $$
  Double R Diner $

Nightlife:
  The Roadhouse
  One-Eyed Jack's

Where to Shop:
  Horne's Department Store

Local Newspaper:
  Twin Peaks Gazette

and his wife Pixie shortly thereafter. The rivalry continued into the twentieth century, until the Martell Mill was purchased by the Packard family. More recently, Andrew Packard, head of the Packard clan, was presumed dead in a boating accident, only to return to seek revenge on his former business partner, Thomas Eckhardt. Andrew's wife Josie and her rival, his sister Catherine, took over operation of the mill in his absence, along with Catherine's husband Pete, one of the last remaining members of the Martell family.

Visitors staying in Twin Peaks will want to make a reservation at the Great Northern Hotel, located at the top of Great Northern Highway near White Tail Falls. There are over one hundred rooms in this majestic hotel owned by the Horne family. There's usually plenty of activity in the hotel, which is often filled with businessmen and fun-loving Icelandic tourists. Ben Horne, one of the town's most prominent citizens, is also owner of Horne's Department Store, where Laura Palmer and Ben's daughter Audrey worked, temporarily, behind the cosmetics counter. Horne is also involved in some shady business deals, including the ownership of One-Eyed Jack's, a combination casino-brothel located at the Washington-Canadian border.

Twin Peaks is inhabited by some very eccentric folks with some rather peculiar idiosyncrasies: Margaret, better known as "The Log Lady," who never leaves her cabin without her log which has psychic powers; the far-out Dr. Jacoby, the late Laura Palmer's psychiatrist, who is still living in the 1960s; the one-eyed Nadine Hurley, who, convinced she is still a teenager, becomes

For Agent Cooper (Kyle MacLachlan), a visit to the Double R Diner wouldn't be complete without a hot cup of joe served by waitress Norma Jennings (Peggy Lipton).

the star of the Twin Peaks High School wrestling team; no-nonsense air force pilot Major Garland Briggs, whose mysterious disappearance in the woods became a matter of national security; and Benjamin Horne, who goes over the edge when he becomes obsessed with the Southern Confederacy and begins to re-enact Civil War battles in his office.

Dining options are limited in Twin Peaks, but the few eateries available offer some of the finest cuisine in the state. The Double R Diner, located on Highway J, offers the best breakfast in town. Owner Norma Jennings will personally serve you what Agent Cooper believes is one of the best cups of joe and the best piece of cherry pie he's every tasted. For a more formal dining experience in a rustic setting, the Timber Room in the Great Northern offers three meals a day to its patrons, though don't be surprised if you see some of locals enjoying a hearty dinner. Travelers heading in or out of town on Highway 1 may want to stop at the Lamplighter Inn, where Agent Cooper recom-

The autumn chill only adds to the tension between local mill owners Josie Packard (Joan Chen) and her sister-in-law Catherine Martell (Piper Laurie).

Twin Peaks, Washington in Snoqualmie, Washington

The show's exteriors were filmed in and around Snoqualmie, Washington, which rests twenty-eight miles east of the Snoqualmie National Forest. The Double R Diner is actually the Mar T Café, located two miles from Snoqualmie. The Packards' sawmill was the Weyerhaeuser Snoqualmie Falls Sawmill, which has since been torn down. Snoqualmie Falls, which can be seen in the film's opening sequence, is 268 feet high (higher than Niagara Falls). The Salish Lodge was used for the exteriors of the Great Northern. The interiors were shot in the nearby Kiana Lodge.

Did You Know?

Before *Twin Peaks* was sold to ABC, a pilot episode was financed by Warner Home Video and distributed on video in Europe. In the European pilot, Sheriff Truman and Agent Cooper kill "Killer Bob" in the basement of the hospital. In the final scene, a caption reading "Twenty-five years later" appears. The final scene is the infamous Red Room dream sequence (featuring the dancing Man from Another Planet), which appears in Episode 2 of the series.

The individual episodes were not given titles on American television, but they were when broadcast in Germany. The episode in which "Bob"/Leland Palmer is revealed as Laura's killer, #14, was titled "Einsame Saleen" (Lonely Souls).

Once the series was canceled, Lynch directed a feature film version entitled *Twin Peaks: Fire Walk With Me*, which chronicles the events leading up to the death of Laura Palmer. Although many of the original series cast were featured, there are some notable characters missing, including Sheriff Harry Truman, Audrey Horne, Josie Packard, and Catherine Martell. The film, which was hissed by the audience at the Cannes Film Festival, fared poorly at the box office in the United States.

mends the tuna fish sandwich, a slice of cherry pie, and a hot cup of coffee.

Nightlife in Twin Peaks is limited, but there are a few places the locals like to hang out and enjoy a beer. At The Roadhouse, which is popular with bikers, you can listen to the live, mellow sounds of singer Julie Cruise and, if you're lucky, watch a rumble. Men who plan to settle down in Twin Peaks may be asked to join the Book House Boys, a secret men's society devoted to keeping the peace in Twin Peaks. Located near the old railroad depot, their meeting place is literally a small house filled with books. For solving the Laura Palmer case, Sheriff Truman made Agent Cooper an honorary member.

RECOMMENDED VIEWING

To get a feel for Twin Peaks, Washington, you should watch the entire series, which is available on videotape. Here are some of the series' highlights:

- Agent Cooper's arrival in Twin Peaks to investigate the murder of Laura Palmer (Pilot).

- Agent Cooper's dream featuring Laura Palmer and the Man from Another Planet (Episode 2).

- Laura Palmer's funeral (Episode 4).

- Agent Cooper and Sheriff Truman have tea with the Log Lady (Episode 5).

- Agent Cooper and the Bookhouse Boys go undercover at One-Eyed Jack's (Episode 6).

- Catherine saves Shelly as the mill is about to blow up (Episode 7)

- Audrey is taken prisoner at One-Eyed Jack's (Episode 8).

- Agent Cooper rescues Audrey (Episode 12).

Twin Peaks

Premiere Airdate: April 8, 1990
ABC   29 Episodes

Cast

Agent Dale Cooper	Kyle MacLachlan	Donna Hayward	Lara Flynn Boyle
Sheriff Harry S. Truman	Michael Ontkean	Dr. William Hayward	Warren Frost
Josie Packard	Joan Chen	Norma Jennings	Peggy Lipton
Catherine Martell	Piper Laurie	Dr. Lawrence Jacoby	Russ Tamblyn
Benjamin Horne	Richard Beymer	Bobby Briggs	Dana Ashbrook
Pete Martell	Jack Nance	Ed Hurley	Everett McGill
Leland Palmer	Ray Wise	Nadine Hurley	Wendy Robie
Sarah Palmer	Grace Zabriskie	James Hurley	James Marshall
Laura Palmer/Maddy Ferguson	Sheryl Lee	Shelly Johnson	Mädchen Amick
Audrey Horne	Sherilyn Fenn		

Sources

Adams, T.R. *The Flintstones: A Modern Stone Age Phenomenon*. Atlanta: Turner Publishing, Inc., 1994.

Applebaum, Irwyn. *The World According to Beaver: The Official Leave It to Beaver Book*. New York: TV Books, 1998.

Beck, Ken and Jim Clark. *The Andy Griffith Show Book*. New York: St. Martin's Griffin, 1985.

Cox, Stephen. *A Hooterville Handbook: A Viewer's Guide to Green Acres*. New York: St. Martin's Press, 1993.

Bennett, Mark. *TV Sets: Fantasy Blueprints of Classic TV Homes*. New York: TV Books, 1996.

Brooks, Tim and Earle Marsh. *The Complete Directory to Prime Time Network and Cable TV Shows 1946–Present (Sixth Edition)*. New York: Ballantine Books, 1995.

Brower, Neal. *Mayberry 101*. Winston-Salem, North Carolina: John F. Blair, Publisher, 1998.

Chunovic, Louis. *The Northern Exposure Book*. New York: Citadel Press, 1995.

Denver, Bob. *Gilligan, Maynard, & Me*. New York: Citadel Press, 1993.

Fernandes, David and Dale Robinson. *A Guide to Television's Mayberry R.F.D.* Jefferson, North Carolina: McFarland & Company, 1999.

Golden, Fran Wenograd. *TV Vacations*. New York: Pocket Books, 1996.

Groening, Matt. *Are We There Yet? The Simpsons Guide to Springfield*. New York: HarperCollins, 1998.

Hofstede, David. *The Unofficial Companion to The Dukes of Hazzard*. Los Angeles: Renaissance Books, 1998.

Keats, Robin. *TV Land: A Guide to America's Television Shrines, Sets, and Sites*. New York: St. Martin's Griffin, 1995.

Lynch, David, Mark Frost, and Richard Saul Wurman. *Welcome to Twin Peaks*. New York: Pocket Books, 1991.

Mathers, Jerry with Herb Fagen. *...And Jerry Mathers as "The Beaver."* New York: Berkley Boulevard Books, 1998.

McNeil, Alex. *Total Television (Fourth Edition)*. New York: Penguin Books, 1996.

Morris, Bruce. *Prime Time Network Serials*. Jefferson, North Carolina: McFarland & Company, Inc., 1997.

Parish, James Robert. *The Unofficial Murder, She Wrote Casebook*. New York: Kensington Books, 1997.

Pierson, Jim. *Dark Shadows Resurrected*. Los Angeles: Pomegranate Press, 1992.

Robinson, Dale and David Fernandes. *The Definitive Andy Griffith Show Reference*. Jefferson, North Carolina: McFarland & Company, 1996.

Schwartz, Sherwood. *Inside Gilligan's Island*. New York: St. Martin's Press, 1994.

Scott, Kathryn Lee and Jim Pierson, eds., *Dark Shadows Almanac*. Los Angeles: Pomegranate Press, 1995.

Stoddard, Sylvia. *A Companion Guide to Gilligan's Island*. New York: St. Martin's Press, 1996.

Sennett, Ted. *The Art of Hanna-Barbera*. New York: Viking Studio Books, 1989.

Waggett, Gerard J. *Soap Opera Encyclopedia*. New York: HarperCollins, 1997.

Zenka, Lorraine. *Days of Our Lives: A Tour Through Salem*. New York: Penguin Books, 1999.

Websites

Batman
http://www.geocities.com/Hollywood/Hills/7537/

Dark Shadows
http://dev2.darkshadows.com/links.shtml

Dawson's Creek
http://members.xoom.com/seechung/dcreek/main.html

Days of Our Lives
http://www.soapcentral.com/days/index.html

Dukes of Hazzard
http://www.smartlink.net/~dstitz/Dukes_of_Hazzard/Hazzard.html

General Hospital
http://www.soapcentral.com/gh/index.html

Leave It to Beaver
http://www.litb.com/

Mayberry R.F.D.
http://members.carol.net/~palmer/index.htm

Northern Exposure
http://netspace.students.brown.edu/~moose/moose.html

One Life to Live
http://www.soapcentral.com/oltl/index.html

Petticoat Junction
http://www.pjonline.interspeed.net/

Peyton Place
http://member.aol.com/alisnrod/index.html

Port Charles
http://www.soapcentral.com/pc/index.html

The Simpsons
http://www.snpp.com/episodes.html